# Traveller's Tales

## an illustrated journey through Australia, Asia and Africa

**Traveller's Tales**
1st edition

**Published by**
Lonely Planet Publications
PO Box 88, South Yarra, Victoria 3141, Australia
PO Box 2001A, Berkeley, California, USA 94702

**Printed by**
Colorcraft, Hong Kong

**Design by**
Graham Imeson

**This Edition**
September 1985

National Library of Australia
Cataloguing in Publication Data

Jenkins, Anthony
    Traveller's Tales

1st edition
ISBN 0 908086 84 9

   1. Jenkins, Anthony. 2. Voyages and travels. 3.
Travellers — Biography. I. Title.

910'.4

Anthony Jenkins was born in Toronto, Canada in 1951, and currently works there as a political cartoonist and very infrequent travel writer for the *Globe and Mail* newspaper. In between, he attended university, put out two half-assed books of cartoons, visited 55 countries, and neglected to get married.

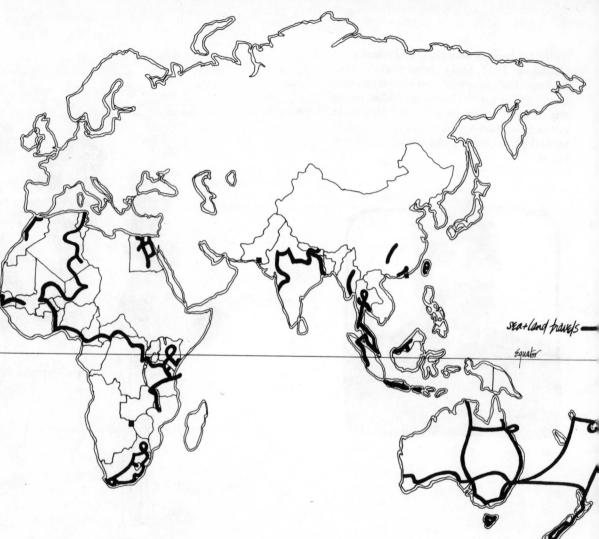

## This Book

This book is a record of travels on three continents in two stints – Asia and Australia from November '78 to March '80, and Africa from October '82 to December '83.

By plane, boat, train, truck, car, bus, bemo, bike, elephant, ass, camel, water buffalo, and on foot through 39 countries – first Australia, New Zealand, Tonga, Fiji, Indonesia, Malaysia, Singapore, Thailand, Hong Kong, China, Taiwan, Burma, India, Nepal, Pakistan, Egypt and Morocco; then Senegal, The Gambia, Tunisia, Algeria, Mali, Niger, Upper Volta, Toga, Benin, Nigeria, Cameroon, Central African Republic, Zaire, Uganda, Tanzania, Kenya, Zambia, Malawi, South Africa, Swaziland, Lethoso, and Zimbabwe.

The Asia route runs roughly from east to west, the Africa route from north to south.

## Dedication

To the people back home who wrote: Mom and Dad, Avis, Larry and Carol. And to my friends from 'the Road': Gordon, 'Gunna', Forrest and Dave.

sea+land travels

Equator

# Contents

# Introduction

I have a photograph on the wall at home that is a favourite. It is myself, on the roof of New Zealand House in London, England, overlooking Trafalgar Square and the River Thames beyond. A Kiwi friend of mine took this picture of The City in moody urban blue-greens, and I am the self-absorbed humanity moving out of the picture to the left. Thick red beard, filthy blue jeans, Nepalese yak wool sweater, and a rolled-up grey balaclava from Darjeeling and latterly, Everest base camp.

'I'd forgotten how it was,' my friend had said when I'd met him earlier that day. ' . . . the Road.'

We'd first met in Sumatra, and later by chance in Singapore, both travelling South-East Asia towards India and ultimately, London. He was now settling into a stay in the UK to try his luck as a photographer.

And 'how it was' was how I am in that photograph. Thoughtful; shabby; seasoned; happy . . . at home.

'Home' is here now, where the photo hangs and from where I write these words. But for that moment 'home' was there, the rooftop of New Zealand House. Or the terrace of the Bozo Bar in Mopti, the Mountains of the Moon, Uganda, or waiting for a lift on the side of the road to Nkhotakota. Home was the Road.

This, for me, is travel.

*Anthony Jenkins, Toronto, April 1985*

6

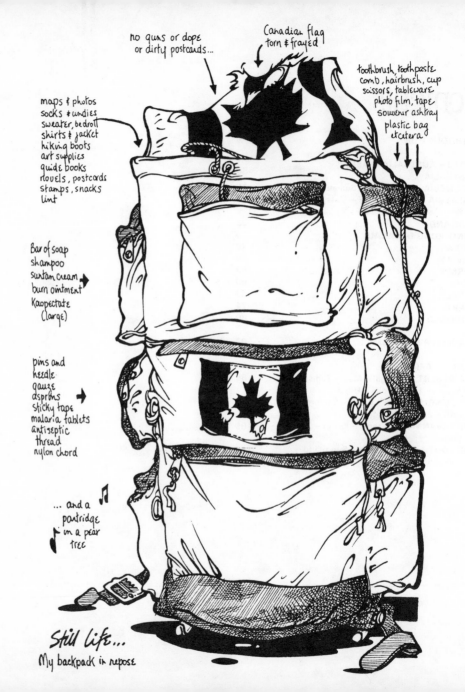

no guns or dope or dirty postcards...

Canadian flag torn & frayed

toothbrush, toothpaste
comb, hairbrush, cup
scissors, tableware
photo film, tape
souvenir ashtray
plastic bag
etcetera

maps & photos
socks & undies
sweater, bedroll
shirts & jacket
hiking boots
art supplies
guide books
novels, postcards
stamps, snacks
lint

Bar of soap
shampoo
suntan cream
burn ointment
Kaopectate
(large)

pins and
needle
gauze
asprins
sticky tape
malaria tablets
antiseptic
thread
nylon chord

... and a
partridge
in a pear
tree

Still life...
My backpack in repose

# Australia & Asia

Australian Travellers - Indonesia
His & hers backpacks and all the
accoutrements of life on the road.
Suntans & sandals, beards and bracelets
(he) unshaved legs and braless (she).
Balinese batik skirt here, Fijian
amulet there. Passports full of visas
and a map full of destinations.

# Australia

My travelling life began 'Down Under' where there are about 40 things that can *end* life – funnel-web spiders, 'box jellies' (jellyfish), uppity water buffaloes, stinging coral, stinging trees, tiger snakes, great white sharks, great thick Queensland policemen, the Mount Isa Murderer (of lone hitchers) and the lethal-looking 'floater' (a meat pie floating in a bowl of pea soup smothered in ketchup).

I travel impersonating an Australian road worker (only without the shovel to lean on) – tanned, frazzled sun-bleached hair, shorts and boots.

\* \* \*

Beer *is* Australia. Men, women and children drink it all day long. One cools one's tinnies in one's Esky, drinks middies, ponies, pots, schooners, and Darwin stubbies in the pubs, 'ladies bars' and leagues clubs. If you are odd and don't drink beer, you are a 'poofter' or a 'derro' who drinks 'red Ned' from brown paper bags. It's a man's life battling to be a mate to his mates and not alienate the 'dragon', one's wife.

\* \* \*

I spent a merry Christmas in the South Australian summer sun. Not a photogenic 'White Christmas' but enjoyable despite its differences.

One in three in Australia works for the government. One in ten is unemployed. At times it is difficult to tell which is which. "Road works" is a bit of wishfull thinking that occupies a good few. Suntanned gladiators in an arena full of potholes. Never in the history of man have so many taken so long to do so little.

Tea boy 'Boiling the billy'

Some of the varied ways of announcing 'Not finished yet mate maybe next year.'

Road 'work' crew, Queensland Australia

Actually, it was one sixth of a communal Christmas that I spent with fellow homeless travellers who found themselves together on Christmas Eve in the YMCA awaiting Father Christmas and various buses out of town.

There were the Laurel and Hardy Germans, out for a month's holiday and a few laughs. Gordon, a sensible Scot looking for money from home to see him through New Year and eventually through to Hong Kong where we would meet for further adventures. A brassy Australian, just out of jail and looking for trouble. A melancholy New Zealander, and yours – Canadian – truly. A dormitory United Nations in shorts and T-Shirts.

We spent Christmas Eve getting to know each other over some souvenir flagons of Australian grog the Germans had bought on a local vineyard tour. It had a nice mock-German name and hit like a Panzer division.

Sentiment flowed and we compared Christmases back home; who would be doing what if we were with our families for the holidays instead of in bunks A, C, E, D, F, and G, Adelaide, Australia.

'Christmas is not Christmas without snow' – a dormitory debate resolved itself four in favour, two in disagreement (Australia, New Zealand). Some people will never know what they are missing. We slipped off to sleep and visions of sugar plums (fermented) danced in our heads.

The Fred and Ginger of sugar plum dancers were in their grand production number when Christmas arrived. Eight am

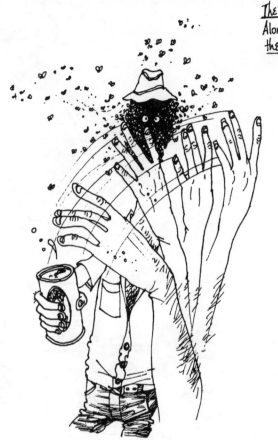

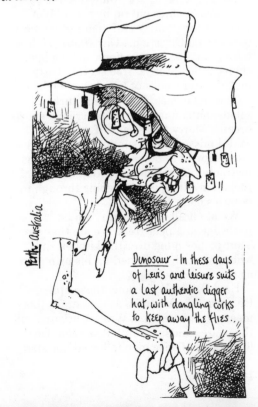

The Great Australian Salute
Along with beer drinking this is the national pastime. A backhanded swipe at a fly or flies. Endless variation on same along with endless flies Often accompanied by individual forms of 'body English' or perhaps more appropriately 'body Australian'.

If the collective energy expended in this practice were utilized for paving the roadways Australia would be in the running for best country on earth....

Dinosaur - In these days of Levis and leisure suits a last authentic digger hat, with dangling corks to keep away the flies..

and the cleaning ladies entered, shouting and bawling like cattle drovers. 'Everybody up!' They were anxious to be through with their duties and be off home where, presumably, their hubbies and kids still slept in peace with their own sugar plum visions.

Idling, we whiled away the time, this one then that rising at intervals to phone home. Each of us in a different time zone, home for those few minutes. Still yesterday in Canada and a family Christmas eve; crisp daybreak on the Scottish moors; breakfast in the Fatherland. We awaited a free Christmas dinner put on by the YMCA. Well, we *were* young and men but no more than casual Christians. Christians? Hell, we were more like hungry lions, licking our chops anticipating a 'free scoff'. 'Tasty tucker' after weeks of lean travellers' fare.

The call comes. Food! Ham, turkey, salads, nuts, mince tarts and cream, shortbreads. Merry Christmas! If grace was said, I missed out. I suppose it could have been slipped in before seconds but I was distracted. An animated group of 20 tucked in with gusto, laughing through the potato salad.

We ate it all – 'a guts up'. And a partridge in a pear tree? We ate that too. Taut bellies hung over the kitchen sink where each of us washed up his own plates as requested.

Eat? Drink? We'd done those aplenty. Be merry? In Australia at Christmas this means at the beach; a White Christmas on the white sands of South Australia. Our little band of wise men followed our star

Christmas Day 1978
Glenelg, South Australia

Dreaming of a white Christmas on the white sands of South Australia, temperature mid 90's. An easy Aussie Xmas post picnic on the beach. A santa fat daddy oversees the excavations. The kids, happy pirates burying Christmas plunder. Womenfolk relax and grandad, watermelon tucked under one wing, stares out to sea like a wizened Lord Nelson.

down to the beach, sharing a tram ride with pensioners sucking at plum pudding in their dentures and smiling their 'I've just spoken to my grandson' telephone-call smiles.

It was warm and sunny and so were the faces of the beach holiday makers. Families gathered around cold hamper lunches. Chocolate-faced kids dug up the beach like frenzied gophers. Fat Santa Dads sat back rubbing their paunches, moving only to open another beer. Old folks dipped white road-map legs into the sea from rolled-up trousers. A carefree casual Christmas.

Our well-fed YMCA United Nations played a six-a-side free-for-all that passed for volleyball against the bronzed beach lifeguards. We were massacred. I hope no one drowned.

Later that evening, back 'home' at the Y with tea and shortbreads and telly (Sabu facing the 'death of a thousand cuts' and we the death of a million calories) I couldn't deny that it had been a Christmas, and a merry one. One that I'll remember long after the Christmas cards start curling at the edges.

\* \* \*

In metropolitan Brisbane I encounter an Aboriginal chap who stopped to admire my sketching.

'That's cool. That's a better thing you've got to do than I've got to do.'

'What's that?'

'Nothing.'

\* \* \*

Reserve Aboriginals

Aboriginal woman

11 Australia

On the nothing outskirts of Alice Springs I met the ultimate traveler. A tatty, bearded old man; almost shy. He had a bicycle pulling a caravan made out of found wood and bits of canvas, plastic and tin. It looked like a big grape on hand-carved wooden wheels. His worldly goods were strapped to its flanks. His plans for Christmas? 'Ayer's Rock, maybe' or perhaps just 'over there', a few metres away by a dead tree.

\*   \*   \*

Except for the snakes and spiders, the lizards, bull ants and termites, scorpions, wasps, bush flies, birds and beetles, we were alone. On all sides, sand, scrub and boulders. Razor vines and stinging trees. Driving ourselves onward in the scorching heat of midday. Lifers escaping from Devil's Island? Almost. We were golfers, enjoying a day on the links at the Outback East Golf and Country Club, Magnetic Island, Queensland. Sentenced to 18 holes, par 64.

Green fees were $1 per round, 'donations appreciated'. I saved my charity for a worthier cause – or course. Clubs could be rented, inexplicably, from the local gas station up the road. A mechanic cum golf pro doled out the niblicks from the lube bay. Tyre irons and seven irons. He kept our watches as collateral.

'Replace all divots' read the score card. Very optimistic. A duffer couldn't raise a

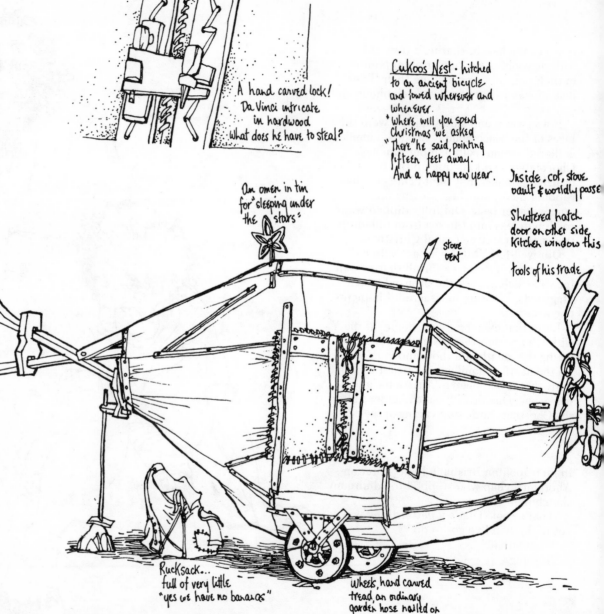

A hand carved lock! Da Vinci intricate in hardwood What does he have to steal?

Cukoo's Nest · hitched to an ancient bicycle and towed wherever and whenever.
* Where will you spend Christmas "we asked "There" he said, pointing fifteen feet away. And a happy new year.

Inside · cot, stove vault & worldly passe

Shuttered hatch door on other side. Kitchen window this

tools of his trade

An omen in tin for "sleeping under the stars"

stove vent

Rucksack... full of very little "yes we have no bananas"

Wheels, hand carved tread, an ordinary garden hose nailed on divot here with an axe. The earth was iron, welded by near year-round tropic sun, and strewn with rocks and sticks. Clumps of long brown grass were nature's afterthought.

On the first tee we ran afoul of the management. All of it. One fellow: course manager, greenkeeper, club pro and bartender. He wore many hats. He also wore a shirt, shorts and knee socks, all of which he less than graciously requested we (stripped like navvies to cutoffs) be wearing. 'This is a bloody golf course, you know!' So we had suspected. Nine holes later, we knew different.

You didn't need a caddie on this course, you needed a camel. Hammering in my tee with a five-iron, I drove into a shimmering sea of heat waves. The 'green' was an island of sand in this mirage, a pock-marked lunar oasis crisscrossed with the tracks of both man and beast.

As this was a 'green' and not a bunker, grooming was permitted. Within limits. Rule No. 2: 'Greens may be scraped in an oblong shape for two metres toward cup'. (Rule No. 1: 'No refunds'.) Any excess of sand or creepy-crawlies could be removed from the cup using the ladle thoughtfully chained to the flagstick at each hole. Local pros (the ones who don't have to be reminded to wear their shirts) have a trick which we quickly picked up. Shuffling up to the pin to survey their lie, they step aside to putt, rolling the ball back along the track they have just innocently furrowed. A little unconscionable strip mining of this sort can shave a dozen strokes off your game.

THIS IS A GOLF COURSE Y'KNOW!

There is no water hazard except the month of January, the rainy season, when more than 300 mm a day is not uncommon. As it is exceedingly difficult to breast-stroke with a nine-iron between your teeth, most serious golfers give this month a miss. For that matter, most serious golfers give this course a miss.

Spray-bombed arrows on boulders pointed us through this nine-hole land of the lost. I lasted seven, and headed for the club-house, where air-conditioned, paid-in-full members, full of beer sat watching television – Jack Nicklaus led the field by four strokes in the Australian Open from Melbourne. They all wore regulation shirts and wide gassy grins.

I wiped the grins off their kissers.

'You shot a 69!' (For seven . . .)

'What's yer handicap?'

To that I had only to look out the picture window at that course and smile.

\*    \*    \*

I don't recommend the red dust in the Ebeneezer Road House out in the Never Never, near Ayer's Rock. Tastes awful! Still, I was fortunate enough not to be in Banka Banka for the 'Top End Wet' when the roadwork becomes swamp reclamation.

I visited Surfer's Paradise where the surf is lousy, and Curl Curl where they say it's fine; hitched to Perth along the Gunbarrel Highway across the Nullarbor Plain with 19 tonnes of frozen kangaroo meat, napping beside the 'Road Train' truck with a bunny warren for a pillow; crossed the Outback

14 Australia

Snakes in the grasslands

Road trains; transport lorries on the Track, south from Darwin during the wet season. Treetop tall powerhouses lugging up to four double deck trailers.

An awsome deisel serpent, snaking through the doorhandle igh speargrass. Time its only natural enemy.

Like all snakes, lifeless and ugly when at rest. Rolling they are frightening, majestic.

by bus mowing down pugnacious roos and stopping at one-horse towns with dogs and drunken Aboriginals sunning on the sidewalk in front of the only bar; caught the one bus a week out of Sand Fire flats (Thursday, 8.30 pm) I've been through Burnt Shirt, Wagga Wagga, Iron Knob and Cocklebiddy, through what the government calls 'Areas of Potential Development'.

And yes, I saw the Sydney Opera House where 'floaters' are never served.

\*   \*   \*

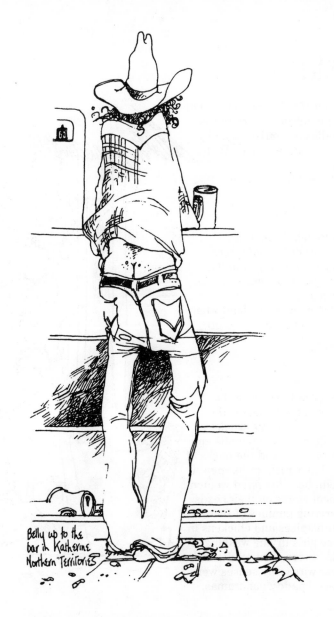

Belly up to the bar in Katherine Northern Territories

# Indonesia

According to rumour the floaters on Legian Beach, on my first night in Bali, were the disembowelled bodies of tourists slain by kris (wavy ceremonial knife) gangs. Welcome to Asia.

'Where you go?' the little kids say.

\* \* \*

Diary Note, Kuta Beach, Indonesia.
*. . . talk of some sort of festival where a live cow is thrown from the cliffs into the sea this Saturday . . . Cafes serve magic mushroom omelettes for tea!*

Who needs hallucinogens in a land where garland-hung holy heifers are hurled off cliffs?

\* \* \*

Bali, Java and Sumatra I saw from the backs of motorcycles or hanging off the backs of 'bemos' (small covered trucks bearing laughably huge loads of goods and passengers); from ox carts and the backs of buses waiting for 'The Crash' to happen. I saw duck herdsmen, bare-breasted women balancing department stores on their heads, motor scooters carrying families of five. Markets stifled with spices and chickens in wicker bells, village girls drying washing on the roadside banks under giant spider web clouds in the power wires. My senses were assaulted by terraced paddy panoramas

Bali — INDONESIA
a small family food and drink stall by the roadside

They do scant business, but abound in the islands. Free enterprise.

with green volcanoes rising in the background. On the roadsides of Indonesia are bird house-sized temples on sticks where little offerings – incense, rice cakes and flower petals – are made. In the full-scale temples, the official crumbling corner ones, beggars and dogs and greedy gods sleep.

\* \* \*

Out in the monkey forest beyond Denpasar, kids catch dragon flies on honey-stickied reeds and eat them alive.

'Hey mee-ster,' they yell, practising their English. 'Where you go? What you want?'

'A big glass of ice water, an air-conditioned room, and a woman, in that order,' I answer. Asia is a thirsty, hot and lonely place.

\* \* \*

It had been a most pleasant South-East Asian day. Seven of us from three continents had hiked the jungle trails down to the shores of Lake Maninjau. We had taken a breather over tea and biscuits at the little village warung, then a refreshing dip, swinging out over the lake Tarzan-style. But somewhere along the line someone must have offended a jungle god . . . one with a sense of humour.

First came the jungle rains. We changed from wet swimwear into wet travel togs much to the entertainment of the little boys who appeared out of the rainy nowhere. They crowded in around us, all in line abreast under the eaves; tall white west-

A becak. (bet-juh)
An Armada of Pedal powered taxicabs plys the sea of humanity on the Javanese byways

Mobile Restaurant. →
A full course meal coming to a curbside near you. Strong back and weak soup. Over 19-billion (flys) served.

soup tureen

foodstuffs

Cash bin
Condiments

breads, cakes

dishes

kitchen utensils

spare coal & oil

dish water

hot coals

The Wheels of Industry
ROAD TRANSPORT - INDONESIA
On the streets of Yogyakarta in central Java an exotic assortment of energy saving uehicals. Some inspiration, some mostly perspiration. Not for show. Just for GO...

YOGYAKARTA A. Jenkins

A two-wheeled tanker.
He was transporting either coal oil or soup. Your guess is as good....

Cement Truck →
(BC)

erners and little dark Sumatrans. We looked like a piano keyboard.

During a slackening in the downpour we sprinted down the road to the shelter of a small cafe. Hot tea, home-made ginger biscuits and passing buses with rooster tails. We roused ourselves and waved down one of the multi-coloured rattle-trap buses. We piled aboard.

Ten minutes later we piled off. End of the line. A short way down the track, the driver stopped and parked in his village, through for the day. No amount of coaxing or pleading would persuade him to take us the remaining 28 km to our beds in Bukittinggi. Well, not quite any amount. He had in mind 10,000 rupiah – about $20 each. Not much by western standards but a king's ransom in Sumatra, where bed and three square meals a day might set one back $2. We regrouped under another set of eaves. More piano keys. Bus after bus rolled in and parked. One of us would dash into the downpour to negotiate a ride home. No dice. There was either a very strong union or a powerful god at work, for not one driver could be persuaded to move. No more buses until tomorrow – except for 10,000 rupiah.

Then the vengeful god must have blinked. We found a van driver hauling damp sacks of rice in our general direction who, it seemed, might bargain, so we loaded ourselves in with the sacks. They say every man has his price. After heavy bargaining this chap's was 8000 rp. Out of the van and back under the eaves, a keyboard no longer as we were gathering a sizeable

Anthony Kerkins - Denpasar, Indonesia

Triumphant... A winning owner parades the victor. Losers lay in the dust.

a tout

Urchins peddle everything and anything; smokes, drinks, eats, hats, postcards. They slice through the throngs where adults can not pass, their wares on their heads.

A wager won, a punter savors a clean kill.

The wagering is fast and furious and **LOUD**. Bettors shout their odds and favorite waving wads of notes, fingers acting as tote boards. Shirts & shoes are wagered. Wadded balls of money are thrown between patrons. Theatrics. Organized chaos. Everyone smokes....

The handlers caress their fighters, soothe them. Love them.... The cruelty comes later

The Killing blade fastened to the left spur

bright linnen wrapping

A handler sings his birds praises to skeptical bettors, coaxing up the odds...

fighting stance

BALI, INDONESIA

Cockfight.

Cockfighting is not the sport of Kings. It is a way of life (and bloody death) in Indonesia, particularly in the villages. Poverty and cruelty go hand in hand...

throng of amused villagers. This was better than TV, which they didn't have in any case.

The law arrived. This was an event of note, for the only thing that moves less than a policemen in Indonesia is a dead policemen in Indonesia. Not that he was much help . . . or any help. He just smiled and smiled. Longer and brighter than a beauty queen contestant. We asked his aid. We asked for a taxi, a telephone, a ride in a police van. We praised his uniform. 'Bagus!' We clapped his back, shook his hand. Finally he conferred with the bus drivers. '10,000 rupiah,' he grinned . . .

Night was falling along with the rain. Wet and becoming miserable, we decided to hardnose our way home. We boarded a vacant bus and would not budge until someone drove us to Bukittinggi. Somewhat taken aback by this change of tactics, the driver put on a tape cassette of what sounded like an Indonesian Yoko Ono and sat behind the wheel refusing to move, pretending to enjoy it. Impasse. Meanwhile, news of the event had spread. Swarms of soggy kids stood outside the bus banging on the windows and cheering 'Sepulah ribu, sepulah ribu!' – 10,000! 10,000!

We couldn't beg, borrow or steal a ride. We certainly weren't going to pay 10,000 rupiah for it. We sat on the bus playing war of nerves with the driver to the tattoo of beating palms and the rhythmic chant of 'Sepulah ribu!'

Suddenly salvation came down that river of a roadway; a truck headed in the Sepulah Ribu direction. I was out of the bus and

Father & son - busride to Borobadur smoking roll-your own (King size)

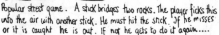

Popular street game. A stick bridges two rocks. The player flicks this into the air with another stick. He must hit the stick. If he misses or it is caught he is out. If not he gets to do it again.....

YOGYAKARTA

Cigarette butt picker-upper, working the streets with oversize tweezers...
(He didn't smoke)

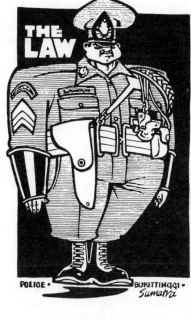

THE LAW

POLICE · BUKITTINGGI · Sumatra

KIDS TOY....
A TIN CAN ROTATING ON A BENT NAIL. THESE ARE WHEELED CEASLESSLY THROUGH THE STREETS. FILLED WITH STONES THEY FRIGHTEN DAYLIGHTS OUT OF THE CHICKENS MUCH TO THE DELIGHT OF THE KIDDIES...

☆ a Satisfied Customer ☆

200 Rp
about 40¢

Street barbers work · Bukittinggi - Sumatra

Things Indonesian
This and that from Bali, Java & Sumatra

19 Indonesia

into the road lickity split, stopping the truck with a dripping Statue of Liberty pose. 'Bukittinggi?' Nod? Smile. Six eager travellers came charging through the storm, like kids on Christmas morning. We huddled ecstatically together in the back of that open gravel truck, half under a leaky bit of plastic. As we left the village, a hundred hypocrites cheered our performance.

The ride home was spectacular, winding up the 'forty-four majestic hair-pin bends' the guide books foretold, numbered in countdown sequence. We rattled around the truck like peas in a drum, taking in cloud-shrouded lake panoramas in the falling rain. We started to sing national anthems (we were Dutch, Australian, German, New Zealander, English and Canadian).

We crested the hill at No. 44, leaving the lake and daylight behind. We entered a dark tree-lined corridor, seven ghoulish figures huddled under a slick black tarp in the moonlight; an Edgar Allan Poe vignette. The rains let up and we entered Bukit-tinggi with a flourish, standing and waving at the open-mouthed locals from the back of the truck as if we were leading a parade.

The driver asked where we were staying, then drove on to drop us at our hotel doorstep. We shook his hand, gave him 2000 rupiah and wished him a heartfelt 'Selamat jalan,' – literally 'Good road'.

We changed into dry clothes, had a warming supper and sweet cakes, hot from the street vendor's oven. We slept and I dreamt of an air-conditioned Rolls-Royce.

\*   \*   \*

Kelas III

THIRD CLASS CARRIAGE
YOGYA–JAKARTA NIGHT TRAIN

A moving experience....
Difficult to get to sleep,
a nightmare to stay awake.
The menfolk smoked,
the women snoozed,
the kids and chickens
screamed & squaked.
If you get too tired
just grab a slice of
floor Granny ...
Eleven hours travel
for four dollars, ten.

all
aboard!

Diary Entry.

*Didn't accomplish a great deal today. Planned to make some plans.* – This from Tuc Tuc village on Samosir Island, Lake Toba, where I did little or nothing but rest. Travel is *not* a vacation, and travellers get weary. I settle up with Mama Krista:

*... 2250 rupiah for nine days accommodation ($4.20) and about 6000 rupiah in eats, mostly banana tacos.*

But travel is not all beer and skittles.

*... Pangururan – Pig City! Big and little black pigs in a grotesque little town. Booked in at Richard's, the only place in town. Had a swim down by the wrecked boats in the canal. Grazing water buff everywhere, big mean-looking bruisers herded by school girls with sticks .... Ate and rested and did a few sketches in the cafe. Just about fractured my skull slipping in thongs on wet pavement, landing on my head. Power failure too. Bed by 9 pm but didn't sleep 'til midnight – noisy place. Pig fights outside, dogs barking and the whole place shaking like its being dismantled. Lying wet and cold and tired in the dark in Asia is no fun.*

*The bus trip from Bukittinggi was 17 hours. Not quite as bad as was made out, but no picnic.*

\*   \*   \*

Self Portrait in God's own country, Lake Toba northern Sumatra.
On to Malaysia....
21/4/79

# Malaysia & Singapore

A becak (three-wheeled motorized taxi) took me to Medan airport where a winged becak completed the journey to mainland Asia.

Temples and mosques. The Indian and Chinese element gives Malaysia a different feel; more prosperous and urban. There are Malays there too, villagers spread out on the roadsides observing god-awful road smashes. The kids now say, 'Hello, John' but 'Where you go?' seems universal.

\* \* \*

Hill stations are British colonial mountain retreats. At Maxwell Hill, jungle Indians boarded the bus wearing shirts but no pants. At the resort restaurants of the Highlands, it was a different scene. I dined with a group of boozing Malaysians – not Malays, they served the meal – but Chinese and Indians. We ate 'steamboat', an entertaining do-it-yourself meal with a constantly boiling cauldron to which we added our own ingredients, calves liver, egg, squid, vegetables, fish. Excellent! Choose you own pace and add what and when you wish. I acquired the art of eating with chopsticks.

We talked of multi-culturalism in Malaysia. There is little. There is great separation of the races. 'Give me a Chinese boss and Malay subordinate any time,' said an Indian chap. They drunkenly related the old joke

IN MALAYSIA

PLEASE REMOVE CRASH HELMET

DO NOT SPIT

Helmet rules are exempted in the case Sikhs ( the turban just wont fit it seems...)

Rules of the road in Malaysia require motorbike riders to wear helmets. There appears to be an unwritten rule that the larger ones head the smaller the helmet worn to protet it...

Fashionable young women will often wear lan old shirt backwards to int unfashionable city gri and grime.

DI-TEGAH · MELUDAH
Please Do Not Spit
தயவுசெய்து செத் தப்பாதீர்காது

Spitting on the bus in Malaysia it frowned upon... in English, Malay, Indian (Tamil) and Chinese.

Outside the Godess of Mercy Temple- stand innumerable misfortunates beg and two huge iron burners, stoke baseball bat sized sticks of incen Backyard barbecue on a grand sc

Pawn Shop Guard - Penang.
Low calibre men with high calibre wepons. They also serve who only lounge and wait....

a way with words....
Armed with a better education and a battered t/pewriter, a street corner writer.
For a fee he'll write letters, fill in forms, write petitions or type your resignation in double space.

STREET CORNER - KUALA LUMPUR

shark fins

IN THE FISH MARKET

Heavy weight champion weigher-in-chief. He hooks up your wicker work platter of shark fins or squid, counter balances with a weight on the other end of his scaled pole and assesses the weight and according price... all in a moment. Subjective, but no one argues.

BEGGAR BURNER

22

about the brain supermarket: Chinese brains 'very used', Indian brains 'slightly worn' and Malay 'like new!'

Later, at Tanah Rata in the Cameron Highlands, an Indian waiter asked that I might draw him. I did and drew a crowd. The Chinese cafe owner was a decent chap who minded that no one draped too hard over my shoulder or spilled tea on the drawing. I drew him also. The crowd called out 'Malay! Malay!' and I was obliged to draw the Malay busboy to complete the set.

\* \* \*

'Border Clothes' – a Third World phenomenon. Everyday travellers' walkabout clothes, city or jungle, are lived-in shorts and T-shirts, sandals and perhaps affectations of Asia – Bali bloomers, beaded Indian vests, toe rings, etc. When dealing with the bastions of officialdom at border posts or visa offices, it is all long-sleeved shirts buttoned to the neck, long trousers, semi-shined shoes. To be identified as a 'suspect hippie' (Thai embassy term) is to face official disfavour. It's *their* country.

\* \* \*

Malaysian countryside is coastal jungle civilized intermittently by huge rubber plantations owned by Goodyear, Dunlop, etc. On the seashore sit dilapidated fishing villages on stilts – kampungs. In the cities, international commerce by day, but at night, the highrise alleyways and parking

My entry into Malaysia

lots throb with street commerce – immense open-air eateries, carnivals, and clip joints set up under lantern light. I can get peanut-honey pancakes, my fortune told, my enemies cursed, or a powdered tiger penis aphrodisiac. I develop a passion for 'motorbike' (murtabak – a large mutton-curry crepe) but not for the miniature whole-fried squid. You have to spit out the beaks. Colonel Sanders operates up the road for those not so inclined.

I like ice cream. Singapore has ice cream parlours boasting 32 flavours. A pretty little Chinese girl fetched up my double-scoop blackberry ripple. At least I thought she was pretty, I couldn't really tell. She wore a surgical mask, cap, rubber gloves and a little 32 over her heart. My cone was untouched by human hands. After six months of adjusting to some rather un-healthy conditions I wondered if my body might reject anything so germ-free . . . .

The ice cream was delicious but some-thing was missing. Humanity. I would have liked to have seen the pretty face behind that ice cream bandito mask.

Singapore, I found pretty much the same. I know there is a personal human face there, but I've had to look for it.

I looked for it down the lens of a new camera I bought there. I was not the only one. Every tourist leaving Singapore seems to be laden with expensive Japanese hard-ware. You could pick us up with a magnet. Even at the $10 a night travellers' hostel where I stayed, penny-pinching backpackers in $3 Indonesian T-shirts and $1.20 Thai thongs returned to the dorm bearing $1500

cheesecake

blueberry cheesecake

*Specialist* – a peanut butter & honey sandwich street vendor

peanuts liquified    liquid honey

*Dayvilles* – 32 flavors all untouched by human hands.

*Life in Singapore is much the same . . . A double scoop of humanity,* PLEASE.

A sensible soft drink vending practice. The vendor retains the bottle for return deposit. The drinks are sold in neat, easily disposable plastic bags . . .

worth of new camera gear . . . and then went out to Komala Vilas restaurant for a 60-cent Indian meal.

That is one aspect of Singapore; shaking hands with your neighbour in an Indian eatery and feeling what you were both eating (properly with your right hand of course) squishing between your fingers . . . or eating in a Chinese food stall and hearing your waiter call the order back to your 'kitchen' in a voice loud enough to be heard in JB (Johore Bahru).

Ice cream mask mentality is in evidence at People's Park. 'Where's the park?' I asked. They must have thought I was pretty dumb. People's Park is a shopping centre.

The mask slips on Bugis Street – a wee-hours side-street circus of transvestites. On Tiong Bahru Road unmasked but *organised* caged song-birds sing sweetly in Sunday morning concert, actually making more noise with their chatter than the old Chinese gentlemen looking on. Quite an accomplishment!

Singapore is a city of signs: Welcome to Singapore, $500 fine, No Spitting, No Sitting, No Littering, No Tittering, No Parking, No Larking, $500 fine, $500 fine, $500 fine . . . .

I liked Singapore. I am selective. I'll remember the shoppers but not the shops, the street operas but not the streets. The sky-gazing fortune tellers and not the skyscrapers. The pretty eyes above the ice cream mask.

\*     \*     \*

Sunday 8ᵃᵐ Bird Concert – Owners arrive with their birds sit back, eat and drink a little, relax and talk to their friends . . . so do the birds . . . .

Sibu (Sarawak):
*... Cleanliness Week Parade. Marching bands and civic dignitaries and broom-toting service tradesmen march through town as part of a huge government-sponsored hygiene campaign. They dump the swept up filth into the canal afterwards.*

\* \* \*

Q: What has 400 eyes, chickens and smiles?
A: An Iban longhouse.

The Iban are tribespeople from the up-river jungle country in Sarawak in Malaysian Borneo. In bygone days they were headhunters and as a result did not have many unannounced visitors drop by.

Times have changed. These days the only heads they might hunt would be those on bottles of Anchor beer brought upriver by rasping turquoise barges. These boats also bring groceries, mail, hardware and the rare adventurous traveller.

Longhouse Tanjong Ng Sebetong is about seven hours upriver on the Balleh, a tributary of the mighty Rejang that cuts through torpid midland jungles and dumps its warm brown syrup into the South China Sea. The longhouse is a village self-contained: one large plankwork warehouse raised on stilts along the riverbank, home for about 300 people. Everyone living there is cousin, uncle or sister-in-law to everyone else. There are individual family units partitioned off inside, but neighbour and family are almost synonymous and no door is closed to anyone.

Nor were they closed to me. I arrived on

They swept the streets spotless and then dumped the refuse into the canal

River taxi
KUTCHING-SARAWAK

that week's riverboat unannounced but not unwelcomed.

Certainly not unnoticed. A stranger had come. A *stranger!* Everyone ran and stared, especially the children. I stood knee-deep at the riverbank in a sea of goggle-eyed children; a freckled novelty in a brown pudding of giggling, gawking kids. They came cascading down the tiers of tot-sized steps leading from the longhouse. I led the parade up and was offered the hospitality of someone's home it seemed, as the place was filled to capacity.

I sat crosslegged in the centre of the room and stared into more poached-egg eyes than a short-order cook at breakfast. Everyone was smiling and giggling. I had not a word of their language so I just smiled back. We all sat grinning for about 10 minutes just waiting for something to happen. 'What next?' We'd have made a fine toothpaste advert.

Finally a schoolboy broke the ice (ice! –it was 45°C in there!) with his third-form English. He was Ballai. He introduced one tittering beauty as his mother. Then he introduced two others, also giggling, also his mothers. He had two sisters and four brothers or five sisters and three brothers, and a grandmother (only one) whom, he assured me, was dead and could not attend.

She was the only one who couldn't. It was standing-room only under the corrugated tin and thatch, mostly kids, women and grandads. The men were off for some time on a hunt (wild boar, deer and monkeys – not heads). Communication was slow but friendly. Overly so. Ballai would answer

IN LONGHOUSE TANJONG
NG SEBETONG

'yes' to every question he did not understand. He didn't want to disappoint – a common Asian trait.

The house was not wide, but extended 30 metres back to a larder and kitchen full of pots simmering on a log fire. We were in the parlour up front sitting on rice mats – huge clean 'company' rice mats that one of the mothers had rolled out. Other mats lay rolled against the walls, bedding for Ballai and his random brothers and sisters. Ma and Pa slept above in a loft. The walls were unpainted wood shined by bodies and enlivened with memorabilia – fading snapshots, totems, a religious calendar left by missionaries.

The Iban themselves are a tiny dark-skinned race, often strikingly beautiful. They remain unlined into old age. The men alone are tattooed from throat to ankle in traditional abstract shapes, reminiscent of fish and flowers, first stencilled on their bodies from a carved wooden block handed down through generations. Both men and women have long loops of earlobe in which they wear, on occasion, massive brass doorknob earrings.

I took my leave to wander around the neighbourhood, all under one roof. The houses were aligned, open-doored, facing a communal hallway running the length of the longhouse. Chickens and dogs lounged waiting for supper as did the village elders. I sat with the village headman, and drew his portrait while he posed in uncomprehending solemnity. I presented this to him to the hushed expectations of the assembled Ibans. He nodded admiration, unconcerned

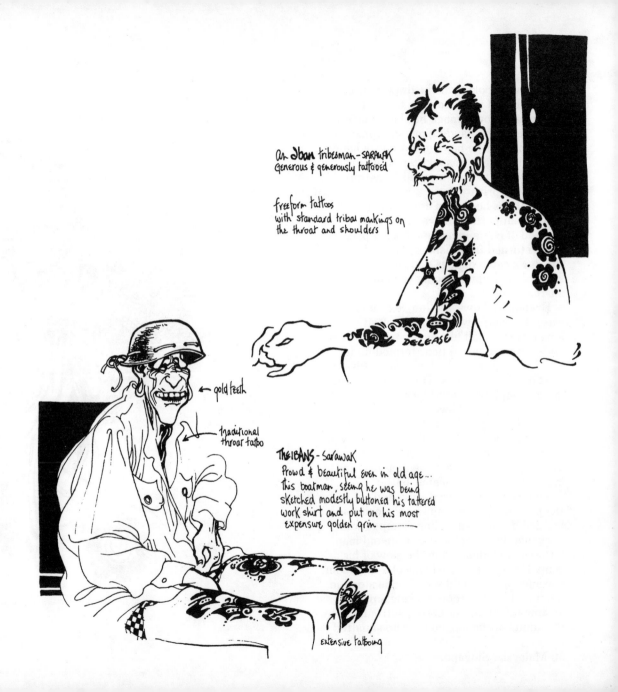

an **Iban** tribesman – SARAWAK
generous & generously tattooed

freeform tattoos
with standard tribal markings on
the throat and shoulders

DELEASE

← gold teeth

← traditional
throat tattoo

THE IBANS – Sarawak
Proud & beautiful even in old age...
this boatman, seeing he was being
sketched modestly buttoned his tattered
work shirt and put on his most
expensive golden grin ———

extensive tattooing

that he was looking at the drawing upside-down. He did not recognise this paper tattoo as his own image but he signalled his pleasure by handing me an orphaned scaly anteater he happened to have handy. I petted it like it was a kitten. It wasn't, and curled into an armoured jockstrap around my privates.

The Ibans howled in amusement.

Near suppertime down at the river a platoon of hosts joined me for a dip as the men returned from fishing. They spread the day's catch on logs and cleaned it, scrupulously apportioning each family's share equally.

Evening fell over the jungle as a pink wash. Oil lamps were lit and dotted the long common hall like an airstrip. Chickens and pigs were put in pens formed under the floorboards by the longhouse stilts –the next meal's death row. Dinner was an oil lamp 'company' affair: black tie, barefoot and glistening with sweat after numerous teas and straight shots of a vile firewater called tuak around a huge common bowl of curried fish and prawns. I offered an exotic dessert; it was for everyone their first and last encounter with peanut butter.

The meal was cleared away and the sleeping mats rolled out. As the children bedded down in snuggling clumps I was beckoned by a bent and sombre old man, tattooed and ghoulish in the glow of his lamp. He led me to the home of a neighbour, a women whose child was ill. She stood in the middle of the room rocking a pale-looking infant on her bosom surrounded by the adults of the longhouse who squatted

Tanjong Ben Osad – HEADMAN
LONGHOUSE NG SEBETONG

againt the walls of the longhouse in mute sympathy.

They imagined I could do something. A Lord Jim scene. I could amuse, I could intrigue, I could smile, but here I could do nothing. I hope that she grows and is well and has her day of giggles and peanut butter with some stranger in days to come.

\*   \*   \*

Boat people. The hulk of a Vietnamese refugee boat is washed up (purposely crashed?) on beautiful Chendor beach. It is full of holes, fish, rice, and shit. Fifty metres away, its 300 passengers sit in a barbed wire-encircled camp watched by Malaysian soldiers while the government figures out what to do with them. The soldiers traffic food and liquor for bribes. A few letters are smuggled out for me to post.

At night (cloudy and moonless nights only) giant sea turtles crawl onto the beach to lay their eggs, returning to the sea at dawn, leaving churning tracks.

A Club Med is being built at the moment, back behind the trees.

\*   \*   \*

REFUGEES! OH WOW MAN WHERE'S THEM CRITTERS AT!

Tourist ON HEARING THAT VIETNAMESE ARE ENCAMPED NEARBY

KAMPONG HOUSE

# Thailand

'Khrap' means yes in Thai.

Thailand is flatter and more cultivated than Malaysia. Water buffalo stand around in rice paddies berated by men yelling 'Fah! Fah!' or 'Ohi! Ohi!' The people are small and neatly dressed. This serves to highlight their difference from me. I've been on the road eight months, sporting a dark, hairy and grizzled look. Small children burst out crying at the sight of me. It's 'Hello *Joe*' here. Thai-sized seats on buses and trains contort me. The Thai alphabet is indecipherable so I stick to 'cow fat' (khow phat) on the menu – fried rice with an egg on top. Travellers eat so many eggs they don't bleed if cut. The heat and afternoon rain force me into midday siesta, native style.

\* \* \*

'Where's the man with the whip?' thought I. You know, the large and sinewy fellow in sadistic grin and loincloth who keeps things moving on a slave galley. In the guts of a ferry with four-foot ceilings and sea slashing in through the viewports it was not difficult to envisage someone tickling my backbone with a cat-o'-nine tails and snarling 'Stroke! Stroke!' I could only be content that my wallet hadn't taken a beating.

The island of Koh Samui lies four hours off the coast of Thailand in the Gulf of Siam. It is coconut groves and beaches and

TRI-SHAW

BANGKOK has many & varied street vendors Here's one I'd LIKE to see...

Hey mee-ster!

GOOD NIGHTS REST 2 baht – ½ hr.

MOVIE ADVERTISEMENT TRUCK – THAILAND
(ONE OF AN EAR SHATTERING ARMADA)

a tuk-tuk BANGKOK

32

little else. Quiet, beautiful and inexpensive. A paradise, except one must endure purgatory to attain it. Purgatory costs 40 baht first class and 25 baht deck class. It is the night ferry running between Koh Samui and Ban Don on the mainland.

Slumberland consisted of three decks: fair, bad and abysmal. The 40 baht 'luxury' class was the six-foot ceiling top deck, checkerboarded with thin foam mattresses and individual pillows. These cost extra. Quite cosy.

'Not-really-so-pretentious' class was the deck below; bamboo mats and long communal bolsters for sleepy heads. A five-foot ceiling.

'Arrgh, let-me-out-of-here I'll-never-do-it-again' class was the bottom deck, 25 baht. Mats if you were lucky, and a four-foot ceiling. It was fit only for carrying sacks of coconuts (which much of the deck space was doing) and passengers with the sensibilities of a sack of coconuts. Like me. I had arrived late and naive and paid my 25 baht sight unseen. 'How bad could it be?'

I boarded, walking over on a wet and shifting plank between the dock and the ferry riding on choppy seas. 'Rather dangerous, that,' I thought to myself. I wasn't wrong. The girl following fell from the plank like a meteor. The unperturbed crew pulled her and her backpack aboard like they were bobbing for apples. She could have easily been jellied between the hull and the dock's pilings. She was quite shaken, so the captain prescribed a Sprite. No charge. Life is cheap.

BATH NIGHT AT THE VILLAGE WELL.

A satisfied customer...

Modestly dressed in sarongs, men & women draw water from a communal bore and scrub up in the village square. Women scour clothing on the washboard logs and geese slurp up the puddles. No one sings in the shower!...

### Street Games in Thailand

① Coins are rolled down an incline. The most distant must pick up his coin and toss it so it strikes his opponents coin... If this has a point it escaped me!

② A sort of one man badminton; the aim, to keep the homemade 'bird' aloft using only ones feet. No easy feat!

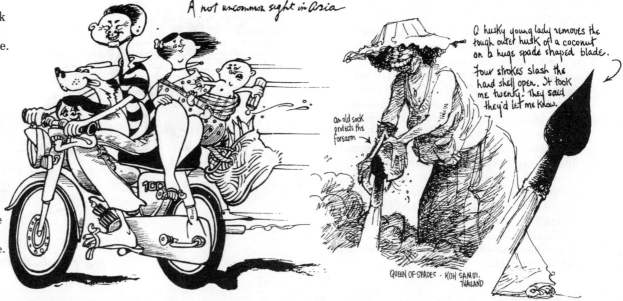

A not uncommon sight in Asia

A husky young lady removes the tough outer husk of a coconut on a huge spade shaped blade.

Four strokes slash the hard shell open. It took me twenty! They said they'd let me know.

an old sock protects the forearm →

QUEEN OF SPADES - KOH SAMUI, THAILAND

We cast off into the night and an eight-foot swell. Soon we were surrounded by a gaggle of smaller boats and much yelling and shouting. Crewmen dashed around the narrow ledge rimming the hull like robot rabbits at the dogtrack. The ferry steamed around in circles. 'Something's up' I thought.

Something was indeed up, and into the drink; a sailor encircled in thick rope struggles through the peaks and troughs towards a tug riding off in the darkness. A dangerous business, and safety is utmost, so as he swims with one arm, he waves a black T-shirt over his head with the other so as to remain visible. The tug is secured to the rope, and the crewman flails his black-shirted way back. To ensure all was as it should be we towed the tug in circles for 10 minutes. I'd always thought it was the tugs that did the towing (as the name implies) but such was not the case.

I went below for some shut-eye, down five steps and back four centuries. A huge roaring engine was caged down one end and a small snoring mob sprawled around on bamboo mats. Everyone's head rested on a central wooden headrest spine from which the sleeping bodies stuck like ribs running the length of the deck, save for the space occupied by heaped bags of coconut. Shoes were neatly filled with sea which sloshed in the large viewports a few feet above the waterline. When these were closed it grew close and reeked of diesel fumes.

I found a fellow soul in torment, an Australian named Rocky, and we stretched out for the night.

**FLOWER LADY** — Threading fragrant flower buds into tiny hanging garlands with which Thai buddists adorn their temples, home shrines, truck mirrors & bicycle handlebars all to the glory of Buddah!

Thai Schoolgirl in standard "sensible shoes"

The only words of English most Asians know
HELLO JOHN!
WHERE YOU GO?

**Thai Scout** white running shoes stained same brown color as socks, shirt & hat

yellow / light blue / pink → / black →

Fish factory worker at Songkhla – a multicolor pungent parfait

side sales of smokes, candy & nuts, etc

Dozens of lottery ticket stalls dot the busy sidewalks of Thailand.

lunch (a durian)

One of Thailand's legions of cart boys

'Do you know what that bug is?' I asked, nodding up at some beetle doing calisthenics on the ceiling.

'Dunno, mate,' he said 'but I've squashed eight'. He pushed out the carcasses with his foot to prove it. 'The sacks of coconut are full of the bastards.'

I shut my eyes and searched for sleep. No use so I got up for a walk. I should have gotten up for a crawl – four-foot ceiling, remember? I didn't. Now I would have to duck a little lower to accommodate the lump. I dabbed on a shoeful of water and went up to the middle deck. It was packed like a New Year's Eve dance floor, only horizontally. A large pyre of luggage lay down one end of the deck. I moved on to the upper deck, the 'stand-up-straight' deck.

It was a westerner's enclave. All the passengers were North American or European backpackers returning from an expedition of indolence on Koh Samui, where living is easy. It appeared, with its mattressed floor and little pillowed groups of loungers, like a Roman orgy by 40-watt bulb. The heavy metal diesel music from below was drowned out by tape-deck Heavy Metal, and any energetic upside-down beetle would have long lost enthusiasm in the dope-laden atmosphere. I had a sudden 1 am-in-the-morning flash of inspiration. I climbed out of an open hatch and up the outside of the boat to the roof.

It was glorious; no crowd, no bugs, and a ceiling to the stars! I stood rocking on that flat tar-papered top deck with the sea breeze lashing at me, alone above all the

← Joss sticks burning

A MINIATURE TEMPLE REPLICA (OUTSIDE A CALTEX PETROL STATION) COMMON RELIGIOUS IKON IN THAILAND.

layers of sleepers like the toothpick sticking up through a club sandwich. I stood there exhilarated in the night, peering back at the waving figures on the bridge of the tug we were still unfathomably towing. I bedded down in the little railed recess above the bridge, and prepared to sleep in the red and green Christmassy glow of the navigation lights. Around me were several lashed-down baskets, a few rolls of tar-paper and a few heavy items, one of which was Rocky the bug killer. (The bugs had won.) 'How yer going?' he said, and rolled over.

I had brought my sleeping bag with me and stretched out in this, head into the wind which caught and ballooned the bag. I twisted and turned and tried to tuck all the folds under my chin but the breeze was relentless and I dozed like a big banana in an inflated skin. Rocky hadn't brought a sleeping bag but had ingeniously rolled himself tightly in a bamboo mat until only his long windblown red hair remained visible. He resembled a lit match. Arranging an orange crate as a headboard, he dropped off to sleep.

In my inflated pocket, I too was dozing when a smiling crewman swung nimbly from the window of the bridge below. 'Fares, please'. It was 2.15 am. Rocky unwound and I deflated and we paid lower deck rates. Hanging by his knees the crewman verified our tickets upside down by the lights of the bridge, then swung off wishing us 'good sleep'.

And this we did have, albeit a short one, lulled by the pitching of the ship and the wind rushing past our ears. The boat

IN WAT PHO - BANGKOK

A monk smoking Marlboros...

In Thailand....
sitting in the temple, it is most offensive to have one's feet pointed at the altar or the monks. Respectful tootsies are always pointed to the rear.

arrived at sunrise, but in plenty of time for us to catch the morning bus to Bangkok.

*   *   *

Bangkok is a perpetual fuming traffic jam amid green-and-orange-tiled temple roofs and golden beehive-domed chedis and wats. Its lifeline (or nightlife-line!) is Patpong Rd, with its bars and bar girls – a splendid time is guaranteed for all. And Ploen Chit Rd VD clinic – a splendid cure is guaranteed for all. Nobody loves you in Bangkok . . . not for less than $10. And every travellers' roost has resident dollies, each 'number one, number one!' according to the Chinese skeletons in undershirts who run the hotels.

Bangkok is so hot and dirty that even the giant Buddhas recline. Their feet are pearl inlaid. Mine are just dirty.

*   *   *

Chang Mai is Thailand's 'Rose of the North'. Northern hill tribespeople wear black, accented with rainbow embroidery, coins, beads, buttons and bobbles. And stoned smiles. This is the 'Golden Triangle', a nondescript meeting of Burma, Kampuchea and Thailand. Heroin-poppy Oz. One doesn't dicker about price – ' . . . but opium is *cheap* here . . . ' – 'So are bullets, man!'

At Kanchanaburi, the 'Bridge on the River Kwai' of Alec Guiness fame, school kids walk bicycles along the track.

In Hua Hin I got a shock. Someone actually straightened my room up! They

YOU WANT WOMAN?

Number 1, Number 1

At one of Bangkok's less respectable hotels...

Patpong

oi, wot vood mama think?

always a number badge

to maintain that eye popping fit constant readjustment seems necessary

— a dutchman joins the act...

Go-going

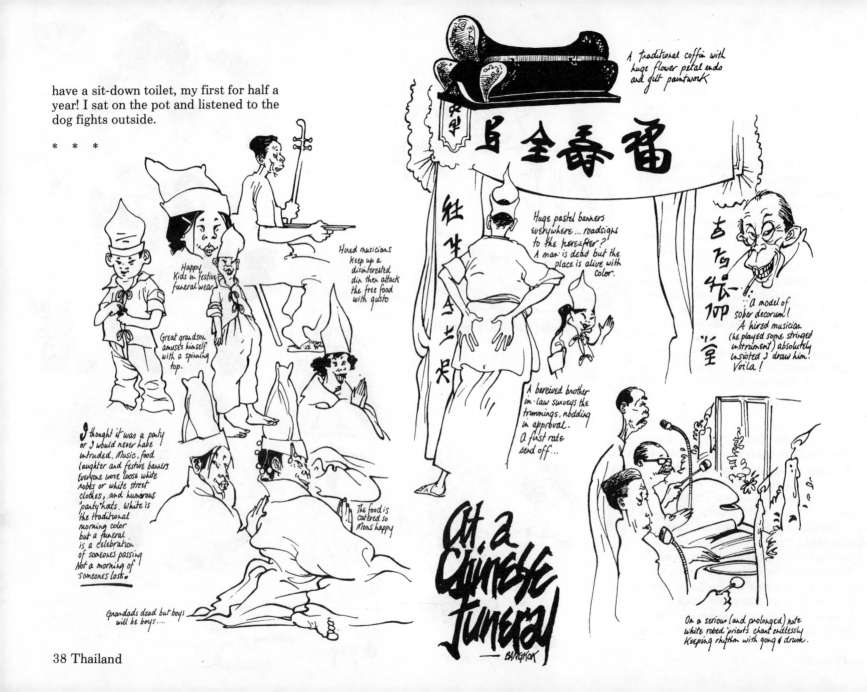

have a sit-down toilet, my first for half a year! I sat on the pot and listened to the dog fights outside.

\* \* \*

A traditional coffin with huge flower petal ends and gilt paintwork

Hired musicians keep up a disinterested din then attack the free food with gusto

Happy kids in festive funeral wear

Great grandson amuses himself with a spinning top.

I thought it was a party or I would never have intruded. Music, food laughter and festive banners. Everyone wore loose white robes or white street clothes, and humorous "party" hats. White is the traditional mourning color but a funeral is a celebration of someones passing. Not a mourning of someones loss.

Grandads dead but boys will be boys....

Huge pastel banners everywhere... roadsigns to the hereafter? A man is dead but the place is alive with color.

A bereived brother in-law surveys the trimmings, nodding in approval. A first rate send off...

The food is catered so Mons happy

At a Chinese Funeral — BANGKOK

A model of sober decorum! A hired musician (he played some stringed instrument) absolutely insisted I draw him. Voila!

On a serious (and prolonged) note white robed priests chant endlessly keeping rhythm with gong & drum.

# Hong Kong & Macau

The rooftops of Mongkok were a sodden Chinese laundry that even the rushing heat from the engines of landing jumbo jets could not dry.

My arriving flight coasted over seemingly endless uniform blocks of flats bristling with bamboo poles hung with Hong Kong's Monday wash.

The streets of Kowloon were overhung with an unending arcade of neon mirrored in wet asphalt. Every business, and Hong Kong is *all* business, hung its million-watt message further out than its neighbour, like jungle plants reaching for the light. These reach for your wallet.

Hong Kong is a rich town. I rested in the lobbies of the big hotels watching the money go by. I asked at the tourist office what to do on a rainy day (a monsoon would be parked off the coast for a week). They suggested shopping.

The Star Ferry got to be my second home, second class. It shuttles between Hong Kong Island and Kowloon, on the mainland. The big island is Big Bucks – international business and finance with street-market finance in the steep alleyways between the skyscrapers. Nature's skyscraper is beautiful Victoria Peak. From the top one can survey the colony. Inland over the world's greatest natural harbour plied by everything from full-rigged junks to the US Seventh Fleet. Over the McDonald's outlets and neon sin bins, the

A REGULAR SIGHT ON THE HONG KONG SIDE OF THE STAR FERRY TERMINAL.....A COLLECTOR OF NEWSPAPERS DISCARDED BY THE MORNING OFFICE CROWD. NO NEWS IS NOT GOOD NEWS IN THIS BUSINESS.

Blind street musician in the Star Ferry walkway

STAR FERRY CREWMAN

flats of Mongkok (reputedly the most populated square miles on the planet) to the Scotland-like New Territories with duck ranches out by the Chinese border.

To the seaward side of Victoria Peak, typhoon shelters with floating acres of sampans, littered beaches, and a litter of rugged islands with dozing fishing villages stinking of shrimp paste drying in the sun, as Hong Kong itself once was.

\*   \*   \*

Hong Kong is a haunt for inhuman urban denizens; people who turn away in the street when asked directions, and who stare back cod-faced in lieu of a smile. A noisy, pushy, hurried place. But never dull, even when a blackout dimmed all that neon.

\*   \*   \*

Nightmare in the Blue Sky Ballroom
*What good is sitting all alone in your room? Come hear the music play. Come to the cabaret, old chum. Come to the cabaret.*
– award winning musical score.
*How much???* – old Scottish saying.

Sitting alone in one's room has many things to recommend it, not the least of which is, it's inexpensive. Unfortunately, it is also often dull, so one night I found myself in the company of two bonnie sons of Scotland in the Blue Sky Ballroom in Hong Kong.

We three (Gordon, Kenneth and I) had

*Gold Miner* – an ear wax cleaner with his assortment of tools.

whisks
tiny shovels

HONG KONG

*Shoeshine* OFF DES VOEUX RD. CENTRAL

been frequenting watering holes of no distinguishable culture. Dumps, some might call them. A Chinese barman uncorking a Pabst Blue Ribbon beer is by no stretch of the imagination a glimpse of the mysterious East.

We were thus keen to experience something exotic, an authentic Chinese nightspot and not one of the glossy tourist replicas such as abound in panoramic swank on the penthouse floors of Hong Kong's international hotels. So we wandered the neon byways with no definite place in mind. We'd know it when we saw it.

We saw it. A couple of pulsing purple palms beneath 100-watt clouds. The Blue Sky Ballroom. We ascended stairs to the third floor above restaurant and shops. Pictures of luscious China dolls, whose inscrutable eyes seemed to follow wherever you moved, gazed out from each landing. The Ballroom was very dark and very cool. A tuxedoed smoothie slid up as if on greased rails.

Being averse to rude surprises, and not being born yesterday we inquired about prices before leaving the black light glow of the doorway. (In Asia generally, 'tourist' is spelled m-o-n-e-y and it is always wise to be forewarned.) Costs were HK$7 a beer (about US$1.35 at that time) and the cover charge was HK$25 from which the cost of the first three drinks could be deducted. Quite reasonable we thought, given the tone of the place. We were escorted to a booth.

The ballroom was comfortable; long and low and dimly candlelit. Plush oval booths

FISHMARKET LADIES
AT ABERDEEN

a band crab
(not at all pleased)

BINDING CRABS
CLAWS - Hong Kong

clung to the windowless walls and sat
scattered in the open like large magenta
clams. A muted orchestra played over a
polished hardwood dancefloor down one
end, and except for the serving staff, we
were alone. The Chinese, we were informed
over the first round of drinks, wouldn't
arrive till after 11. The Ballroom was open
until four. This was fine with us. We'd have
a couple of quiet beers before the action
started.

It *had* started though. A poised and well-
presented lady who we took for around 50
arrived, introduced herself and inquired if
we might not enjoy some company. Female
company. Three charming ladies, it seemed,
would like to make our acquaintance.
'Well, gosh, that wouldn't be bad at all,
would it, fellows? Sure, bring them over, if
you would be so kind.' No one could say
we weren't sociable.

Our fairy godmother left and three fetching
young women appeared and arranged themselves among us. At this point, lest one be
tempted to think us complete rosy-cheeked
simpletons, let me say that we were
expecting a 'catch', a little grey raincloud
to cross the Blue Sky. Probably we would
be expected to buy the girls drinks as is
the custom in gin mills in this part of the
world. 'Lady drinks' these are called –
high-priced watered-down liquor or a shot
of cold tea to be demurely sipped. Perhaps
they were 'taxi dancers', charging a few
bob for five minutes of featherfooting
round the dancefloor.

This was to be our Big Night Out and we
were grudgingly prepared to spend a little

Mah-Jong Parlour
'A MANIA IN HONG KONG'

for the sake of experiences new and unusual. However, we would first chat and go slow and test the waters before casting our hard-earned bread upon them. Basically, we wanted as much as possible for as little as possible. This was always the unspoken understanding between myself and the thrifty pair from Ayr.

The girls, like Goldilocks' baby-bear porridge, were 'just right'; not too hot, not too cool, attentive but not fawning, friendly but not brazen. Charming in every way. Interesting too, but one would have to be able to converse in Cantonese to find out, as only one of them had even a rudimentary knowledge of English. But they were pleasant enough to listen to and easy on the eye as well.

All wore Suzy Wong style silk dresses and discreet touches of make-up and jewellery to bring out almond eyes and alabaster throats in the candlelight. Altogether they were quietly, captivatingly *female* – an endangered species in the western world.

Things were moving along swimmingly in smiling pantomime. We may not have been Diamond Jims, but we considered ourselves not without a certain budget-minded charm. We were in mid charm when our company discreetly produced small pads on which they made a notation and dropped three slips in the holder which contained our cautious bar tab.

'What's that?' we asked in chorus – but it looked suspiciously like bills, in Chinese, for $5 times three.

'Whoa! What's all this then?' Gordon

a slow night in the snake oil business

Palmist — TEMPLE STREET

looked pale and began shaking his head –
one could almost feel the hairs rising on
the back of his wallet. The girls were all
doe-eyed innocence. It struck us like a bag
of doorknobs that these women were to be
*paid* to sit with us! Aghast, we summoned a
waiter to shed some light on the situation.
He couldn't, but brought a fresh bowl of
salted nuts. He was fluent only in international brand names, Smirnoff? Johnny
Walker? Bacardi-Coke?

We nursed our beers and had him fetch
our fairy godmother. The girls were sitting
pretty while we wondered what we were up
for. The sweet bird of innocence had flown
and we could sense mercenary vultures
circling. We began making feeble attempts
to ease the women away. We weren't too
successful – the problem of getting rid of
beautiful women was not one that had
plagued our pasts.

The girls looked at their watches and put
three more slips into the holder. Over the
dance floor red and green Christmas lights
began pulsating and a midget singer in
sequins broke into a high-pitched disco
squall. It was a nightmare! Five dollars for
each five minutes of sitting there! We were
in a taxi, in a traffic jam, with the meter
running! These girls were accountants
without the green eyeshades. They were a
bushfire on the scrubland of our finances!

The godmother appeared. By now we
had shed any pretence of urbanity – 'what's
all this about?' These young ladies were
hostesses, she explained, and companionship
was offered for a fee – $60 per hour. We
could ask them to dance if we wished.

'What! For $60 I'd want them to juggle or jump through hoops on fire!'

It was also our prerogative to send the girls away at any time; did she understand that we wished the girls to leave us?

'Yes!' we cried in brutish unison. They left unruffled and without a goodbye under the wing of the mama.

The slippery maitre d' oozed by. He explained, under arched eyebrow, that such was the arrangement of the Ballroom after the tradition of the Japanese geisha houses. The ballrooms had in fact been introduced during the Japanese occupation of Hong Kong during WW II. Hostesses of high quality were provided by the establishment for the pleasure of patrons. They charged fixed rates. If you wished to buy the women drinks this was extra. If her services were required till closing time there was a flat rate. If one wished to take a hostess off the premises – 'buying her out' this is called – the price was flexible according to how near it was to closing hour. Any other personal arrangements once outside the ballroom were to be made with the lady herself. Nothing was guaranteed, except that it was guaranteed to be expensive.

'A dollar a minute just for talking to us!' gasped Kenneth. 'A dollar!!!'

He could scarcely bring himself to say it, let alone believe it.

'I di'na believe it! Imagine if we were charged the locals 60p a minute just to talk to 'em!' (Kenneth and his brother work behind the bar of their parents' pub in Ayrshire.)

UNLOADING ICE — CAUSEWAY BAY

One does not trifle with the affections of a woman with an icepick between her teeth....

GODDAM HEAT!

GODDAM CABS!

DOORWAY SCENE — HONG KONG HILTON HOTEL

'We ought to charge them a pound just to *listen* to them' mused Gordon.

'Would you like another beer?' asked the maitre d'.

'How much is the bill now? Do the girls come out of the cover charge?'

'Yes, sir' he said, snapped his fingers for the waiter's flashlight beam and tallied all the slips. $105.

'What!'

'Remain calm, sirs.'

He explained: three beers charge, hostess charge, *nut* charge, tax 10%, service charge 10%. All quite standard.

'Be calm, we do not cheat you . . . would you care for another beer?'

We ordered three more. *Beers*. What the hell? By now a few parties occupied booths in the ballroom. Groups of four and five dapper Hong Kong businessmen sat with bevvies of high quality rent-a-ladies un-corking bottles of champagne and slithering around the dance floor oblivious to the mounting minute-by-minute tally. Money was no object.

With the second round of beers our bill came to $128, or $42 a head for just under an hour's diversion.

'An all time record', proclaimed the Scots. 'An all time record!' As if indeed in some great and musty hall in Edinburgh a list of all-time horrific expenses were kept, for future generations to stare at in slack-jawed disbelief.

\* \* \*

The floating Casino - MACAO
Retiring gamblers can have their wagers lowered in baskets from balconies above the tables.

pregnant

Portuguese monk in MACAO

Keno players
LISBOA CASINO - MACAO

The YWCA in Hong Kong is on Man Fuk Rd.

Schoolkids in the New Territories suck on lurid orange barbecued chicken feet and throw the bones out bus windows.

I did not try the 'fungus soup'. 'Duck web', I tried. It was duck feet without the duck, and tasted like sauteed inner tube.

*   *   *

Macau is Portuguese China, a jetfoil ride away from British China, Hong Kong. It is fuelled by the casino gambling losses of little old Chinese grannies, who dress all in black, spit on the broadloom, and are worth their weight in $100 chips. The colony is graced by a leisurely Latin pace on its shady, moss-hung avenidas and South China Sea promenade.

*   *   *

'WINEGLASS' GONG

CYMBAL & GONG

Chinese Priest - MACAO

strongbox!

Blind Beggar - MACAO

# China

Garbage man - 6 a.m., the sun & workmen are rising as the neighborhood trash collector comes down the street, ringing his bell and leading his stunted stallion....

Impressive! China in a word, and not just mine.

I toured the People's Republic with a party of hard-boiled Aussie sheep ranchers and their dragons. Not an effusive lot without a bellyful of Tsingtao beer, but China drew unanimous praise.

China is a uniform place. The soldiers dress in baggy green tunics with a red star on the cap and red trim on the collar. No insignia of rank (I was told this was determined by the number of pockets). The civil guard wear similar, with blue pants. The police wear white jackets and cap with the red star. Railwaymen wear blue caps with star. Visiting Hong Kong Chinese wear advert T-shirts – 'Coke', 'Jumbo Restaurant Aberdeen', 'San Miguel Beer', etc.

\*   \*   \*

In China I was 'guelo' (ghost man) some sort of traditional boogie-man with red hair and beard. In the warren of scrubbed narrow sidestreets adults gaped in amazement and kids fearfully murmured 'guelo'. Even the pigs stared! Honest! I was for most, their first living example of western civilisation in tank top, rolled-up jeans, track shoes and coolie cap. Sorry folks.

\*   \*   \*

Personal Transport for ⅓ the world...

One of a great many on the roads of China

16-07134

I got stares, but not unfriendly ones. My itinerary of cities was enforced but I was free to move anywhere in them. And did.

The principal streets are tree-lined and parks abound. There was little motorized traffic, just work trucks and tractors. The rush-hour streets were swarming with uniform black bicycles. It was charmingly quiet, just the hum of a thousand bike tyres and tinkling bells as they rounded corners eight abreast. There was no neon. Signs advertised motion-pictures or revolutionary do-goodism. There was no litter (in fact, little in the shops with which to make it) and no street scene was complete without a sweeper with his big-wheeled cart.

The countryside was cultivation. No landscape was complete without a work party bending in the paddies. Men and women work equally at any job, although all the 'honey dippers' (those who clean the latrines and ferry the excrement to the vegetable patches in buckets on a yoke) were women.

\*    \*    \*

In a rare moment of luxury I sent my laundry out. It was returned within a day as a neatly starched and ironed pile, on top of which rested a feather and a 10 yuan note. The note was worth about $6. The feather was worth nothing. It just happened to be in my pocket, forgotten along with the money. Of course both were returned to me safely.

I grew to expect the exemplary from China.

\*    \*    \*

A Lady with buckets of human dung...
(Discreetly referred to as "HONEY")

HAND WATERING THE FIELDS ON A COMMUNE

# Taiwan

Taiwan is China too – the Republic of China. (The other billion folks are the *People's* Republic of China.) It has neither the charm or potency of China nor the efficiency and decadence of the west, yet it aspires to both. Its claim to fame is a monopoly on democracy among the Chinese peoples of the earth, and some nice gorges and mountain scenery.

Very little English is spoken and I found myself forever drawing pictures of cows to signify I wanted milk in my tea. The few English conversations I had with Taiwanese were invariably a defence of the existence of 'their' China and a diatribe against the scourge of Communist dictatorship. This, in spite of the fact that Taiwan was run by an unelected President, Chiang Kai Shek's frog-faced son, and an ever-vigilant and annoyingly high-profile military.

\* \* \*

Taiwan's bakers do creative sweet rolls and buns – lizard-shaped buns, frogs, fish, dogs . . . they even do tits. I would not lie about this.

\* \* \*

The taxicab drivers of Taipei are a sad and angry lot of bachelors. They are ex-servicemen who lost a war under Chiang Kai Shek and retreated to Taiwan to find

In Taiwan they go to great lengths to remind you they are 'FREE' and they actually loathe the Communists who, they like to repeat, have their mainland brothers in bondage. (This belief is daily reinforced by heavy media slanting. Yet, the scene below — Taiwanese schoolkids, in military look uniform and mandatory ugly haircuts are paraded into a bus queue by a helmeted little Hitler-cum-prefect . . . .

student name and school no.

217

↑ Bus no.

clip on 'combat' boot look

I'd estimate two in three schoolchildren wear spectacles in Taiwan . . .

They also wear unattractive 'regulation' haircuts as well proving the educational establishment is equally shortsighted.

white knee socks always rolled down

hostility and no wives among the native Taiwanese and hill tribesmen.

*   *   *

I was probably drawing another cow when the fellow at the next table ordered. They brought my tea with milk and for him a cage of snakes. He indicated his preference, and it was whipped against the floor by its tail and hung, stunned, from a coathook by a small noose. Still writhing, it was slit lengthwise with a half scissor, a vein pulled out and drained into a shot glass. Dark thick blood. Down near the tail another incision was made and a little black organ was snipped out and a black fluid squeezed out. The whole cocktail was shaken in a bloody turtle shell and downed in a gulp, chased by a shot of Johnny Walker.

It was an aphrodisiac. I stuck with drawing cows.

*   *   *

Pagodas and temples – Taiwan has a palpable Japanese presence. The island was in fact occupied by the Japanese for a half century up until WW II, and the best of its civilizing influences remain.

It was a nice place to wake up in, a Japanese mountain inn. The rooms were 'tatami' style – cool and soothing to the bare feet, rice mats covered the floors, and light translucent walls could be moved to give a more open feel. A sculpted pool with giant fighting goldfish sure beat TV and the babbling fountain was a soporific

51 Taiwan

full dress twill in 98° heat...

standard eyeglasses Most of the Taiwanese forces seem to have weak eyesight

Ever present govmt. issue smoke

The government has a total monopoly on cigarette and alcohol products. Its army is a prime consumer...

TAIWANESE SOLDIER

I've seen military presence most everywhere in S.E. Asia. but mostly passive strollers & loungers. In Taiwan one sees open, militaristic presence. Jet fighter flyovers. Troop manuevers. Armed guards.

whatever happens they will not be caught unprepared...

Zip sided 'laced' boots

TOURIST POSING WITH MOTIONLESS GUARDSMAN AT THE REVOLUTIONARY MARTYRS SHRINE...

– Taipei

delight at night. I was spoiled by Japanese landladies who catered to my whims and brought endless flasks of tea. I didn't care to bake myself in the scalding mud pools and contented myself with tonic R & R. I had a run of illness and an excess of hard travelling. I must get fit for India.

Throughout South-East Asia travellers sang the praises of the Philippines. A quick look at a calendar revealed it was the rainy season there. So my destination swung west to the Indian subcontinent via Burma. It would be dry there, and assuredly, not dull.

* * *

**BITCH QUEEN**
All malevolent pout and grand, sleeve flapping vanity.

**HEAVY**
But not unlikeable. A lusty, vain and bombastic beard stroking petulant little boy.

**DRONE**
Totally incongruous amid the costumed splendor, these chaps in casual whites walk on in mid scene with props and quiet dignity.

FAIRY PRINCESS

*Characters at the Chinese Opera*

TAIPEI

A SCHEMER

**THE BUFFOON**
A squeaky voiced and wispy bearded little agitator and happy-go-lucky coward. He links the players and action.

# Burma

Burma has seen better days. Tourists may see it for seven days only, and the unofficial price of admission is a bottle of Johnny Walker Red Label and a carton of 555s. Trishaw drivers will pay blackmarket kyat (pronounced 'chat') for these, and the money can be spent on the sweet life in Burma. It's useless elsewhere.

\* \* \*

Dinner at a roadside food stall in Mandalay was chepatis, bean curry, samosas and curd lassi, and prompted me to begin wiping the rims of communal cups and forks with my shirt-tail. This habit eventually left me with a girdle of ptomaine but gave a delusion of hygiene in a continent where it is minimal at best. Like India, Burma is *not* a place to get sick. Or to be squeamish.

It was a fine spicy meal and I told the serving boy so he relayed my compliments to the 'chef' who rushed up, beaming, to shake my hand. He was covered in clusters of purple lumps like mauve tapioca! I wiped my hand afterward, and though street food was often delicious, from that time on I kept my appreciation to myself.

\* \* \*

Candacraig is a beautiful British hideaway. It was built by the British, for the British,

BAGGAGE CONVEYANCE SYSTEM - RANGOON AIRPORT
Installed by the British in the 20's and still going strong —

and its only misfortune is that it's nowhere near Britain but in upper Burma. This is a mere technicality and one which, on the cool tropical evenings of a time gone by, with a brandy and a sigh of satisfaction, one did one's best to overlook. If they couldn't be home, they could jolly well pretend.

The glory days of Empire are gone and the former colony is now calling itself the Socialist Republic of the Union of Burma, but the spirit lingers on gracefully at places like Candacraig.

It is not comfortable to reach Candacraig, but it is easy. And different. Jeeps leave Mandalay – a 12-hour rolling zoo of train ride north from Rangoon – for Maymyo many times daily. The fare is 10 kyat and departures occur whenever a jeepload of passengers is assembled in the central market. 'Jeepload' is a flexible term; it depends upon the flexibility of your ribcage. Ten passengers in six seats is about par. The journey takes two hours and you'll get well acquainted with your neighbours. You get dropped in the main street of Maymyo which sits in the hills overlooking the pagoda-studded plain surrounding Mandalay.

Maymyo is a sleepy compromise, a small picturesque Victorian-Burmese town. It is the old provincial capital of the region. The High St divides rows of two-storey Victorian shops selling spices, sweetmeats, dime novels, and fly-clotted meat. A gaudy pagoda shoulders aside faded examples of whitewashed frame grandeur. In the town square a clock tower in pastel blue and yellow chimes the hours to the same tune as Big Ben.

newspaper

banana leaf filter

Homemade cigar —MANDALAY—

BURMA IS A NATION OF CIGAR SMOKERS.. (AND SQUATTERS)

From the town it is only a short walk to Candacraig. But you do not walk. It is simply 'not done'. Your coach awaits. From almost anywhere in town a dilapidated horse carriage can be hired to carry you in bone-jarring splendour the three km to the rest house.

The signboard out front says 'Maymyo Rest House' but it is still commonly known by its former colonial title, Candacraig. But you won't have to look at the sign. You'll know. It looks just as is should. Around a bend in a very green, very English, country lane of overgrown hedges and ferociously flowering gardens it appears through open gates atop a slight rise. Smallish, turreted, two-storied rusty brick being swallowed in a tide of ivy.

A Burmese flag hangs limp from the flagpole where once the Union Jack faded in the tropic sun.

A groundskeeper in work-worn blues and a pith helmet fans up a breeze with long looping arcs of his grass slasher. During a brief burst of rain he retreats to a small gazebo thick with an icing of vines. Throughout my stay at the rest house he was a fixture on the brick-bordered front lawn, in relaxed but perpetual motion.

A crescent drive and a small sweep of marble portico lead you inside.

Teak. Aged and time-worn teak is everywhere. It is a teak cavern. Twin teak staircases sweep up to a landing. The floors are unbuffed hardwood as are the ceiling, the reception desk and a large fireplace along one wall. Tiny teak figurines of natives in traditional costume stand

KITE FLYING IS AN IMMENSELY POPULAR PASTIME IN BURMA

— in the streets of Rangoon

females waistband snug

males always wear a knot in front

monk with begging bowl & toothpick

along the mantel and mouldering pairs of antlers are mounted high above the entrance. The walls are the same pastel shades as the clock tower in town and cut high up by leaded windows with diamond facets. Glistening spittoons are near at hand. It is from an earlier age, before air-conditioning, colour cable television, touch-tone phones and synthetic charm, and it has none of these. It is beautiful, placid, dignified, and if it was expensive I suppose it would be called stately. It is a traveller's dream, authentic, inexpensive and just a little past its prime.

It has been a rest house for the colonial Bombay-Burma Trading Company's execs, Japanese occupation forces HQ, and Burmese government employees' club (in a socialist people's paradise!). It's now open to anyone fortunate enough to find their way there. These are not many as Maymyo is off the beaten track, as is Burma itself. Burmese tourist visas are strictly limited to seven days so if you do get there your stay will necessarily be short. But sweet.

This history I learned from the inn's front desk man who is not made of teak, but is dark and polished enough to be so. 'Receptionist, clerk (pronounced 'clark'), cashier, storeman, and storyteller.' Mr Kalansuriya is a toothy, charming Ceylonese (not Sri Lankan, please).

'Hello, how are you sir? Oh, yes we have a room for you. We heard you were coming. Will you be having meals, sir? Would you be having English dinner or Burmese dinner? Yes sir, at breakfast also? At seven o'clock? No, no, later to be sure! Even at

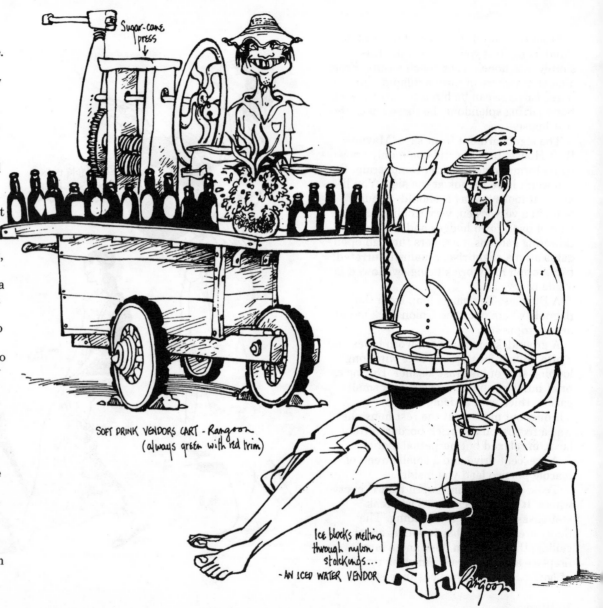

Sugar-cane press

SOFT DRINK VENDORS CART - Rangoon
(always green with red trim)

Ice blocks melting through nylon stockings...
- AN ICED WATER VENDOR

Rangoon

*nine* we will serve you! A boy will take your order. Up there is your room, number 23. If you need any things, you shout to me from there. I am always here.'

My room 'up there', from which there was no need to shout, cost 23 kyat (about $4). It was small but cosy with all one could want without catering to pampered western expectations. A comfortable, canopy double bed with clean sheets, warm woollen blankets and mosquito netting. Underfoot, uncarpeted teak. There was a small table on which sat a flask of drinking water. A single straight-backed chair and clothes rack. Double door with frosted glass panes opened onto a narrow balcony beneath the eaves. Standing here, I looked over the front lawn and gazebo and snatches of red dirt laneway beyond the trees. The grounds-keeper waved up with his free arm.

I was the only guest.

Time eased by. Candacraig is a rest house, a place to get away from it all. There are few diversions laid on. A long walk, a good book, your feet up on the balcony rail with a cup of tea, watching the sunset at your leisure.

I like my leisure particularly leisurely, and awoke from an afternoon nap just in time for dinner.

I had ordered the English meal (about $3). Dress was casual: army surplus (British of course) shorts and a T-shirt. The dining room was small and its walls a flaking powder blue. A vase of marigolds sat on each table flanked by bottles of HP sauce and McIlhennys Tabasco. The HP sauce was inscribed 'By Appointment to Her

WAITER IN A CAFE —
Rangoon

Majesty The Queen'. How should this read in communist Burma? 'By Appointment to the Central Committee of the Socialist Republic of the Union of Burma?' My water glass read 'Tiger' in blue. Courtesy of the capitalist Tiger brewery in Singapore.

Comrade waiter arrived with the squeak of rubber thongs on teak. He was dark, brisk and efficient and wore a salt-and-pepper tweed jacket over traditional Burmese street clothes. He had the cleanest finger nails I had ever seen in Asia. The Empire may have crumbled, but its good habits remain.

Successive courses arrived on silver trays. I had vegetable soup with hard bread and soft butter, a large portion of grilled steak served with roast potatoes, whole carrots, lettuce, and a mystery, torpedo-shaped local vegetable. Dessert was a custard apple, an Asian fruit which looks like the cross product of an apple and a hand grenade.

'Yes, I'll take my tea on the veranda, thank you.' Tea was brought to me there – full silver service on a platter engraved 'Strand Hotel, Rangoon'.

The term 'romantic' to me had always been a plural one. A man and a woman. I was quite alone now in a pool of lamplight under the ivy covered arch of the entrance. All alone and enjoying the solitary romance of the situation. It was cool now, and very dark. It always seems somehow darker at night in Asia. The only sounds were crickets chirping and tea being poured and gently slurped from the saucer,
Burmese fashion, by the groundskeeper

Taxi in Mandalay...

The roadways of Burma are travelled mostly with oxcarts and horsecarriages. The nations luxury transport is an odd assembly of post war autos, Russian SKODAS, 56 CHEVY Bel Airs, immaculate old VALIANTS, EX-army JEEPS and even a powder blue 1954 ← AUSTIN SALOON.

58 Burma

now finally taking his rest. The feeling there was almost spiritual; a reverence for personal peace and harmony. A tape deck or a mug of instant coffee would be sacrilege. I retired early to a fine night's sleep under the mosquito canopy.

I awoke at seven. The day was sunny, birds sang and the groundskeeper was already at work. Mr K bid me 'Good Morning' on the stairs down to breakfast. Double doors opened onto the front lawn. Breakfast was as I'd expected: porridge, toast and butter with dark, tart preserves, eggs sunny side up, sausages and tea.

I had to leave that morning hastening back to Rangoon before the seventh day of my visa. I paid the bill and signed the guest book. Usually this is a nuisance. Here it was a privilege. I spent only a brief time at Candacraig and then returned to the real world. I spent a day and a night, but I could have spent a decade . . . the 1930s.

*   *   *

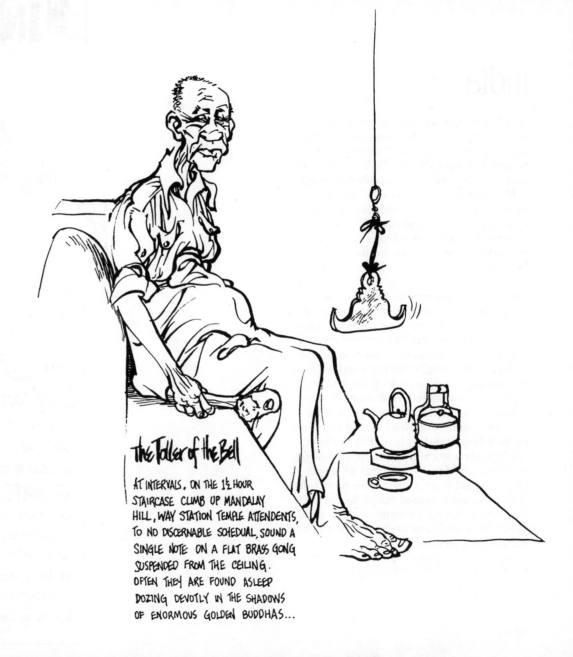

the Toller of the Bell

AT INTERVALS, ON THE 1½ HOUR STAIRCASE CLIMB UP MANDALAY HILL, WAY STATION TEMPLE ATTENDENTS, TO NO DISCERNABLE SCHEDUAL, SOUND A SINGLE NOTE ON A FLAT BRASS GONG SUSPENDED FROM THE CEILING. OFTEN THEY ARE FOUND ASLEEP DOZING DEVOTLY IN THE SHADOWS OF ENORMOUS GOLDEN BUDDHAS...

# India

As I entered India and Calcutta a sign welcomed me. Beside it squatted an Indian emitting an arc of piss. This would be typical. Indians called me 'sah'b' and 'babu' and were charming and wonderful people.

Bombay is 'the money city', London with palms. Delhi is 'the government city'. Calcutta is 'the city of culture'.

Sunday cricketers, white-shirted armies of clerks riding bicycles, herds of holy heifers (little better than giant rats with haloes) who bed down on roadway islands and head for the crowded markets at dawn for a free feed. Curbside dentists, sidewalk scribes, barbers, and boot menders, pavement mechanics, ear-wax excavators and lean-to condos of destitute sidewalk sleepers.

An armless beggar played cymbals with his feet (how did he pick up the change?), a legless torso dragged itself along through Chowringhee, enterprising youths prised up a pavement stone and buried the head of their headstanding leader in the sand. All in a day's work. Calcutta is unendingly repellent and fascinating, and what you might expect from a city whose namesake, Kali, is an eight-armed turquoise tart with long red protruding tongue, a chain of skulls for a necklace, and a disembowelled corpse for a footstool.

\* \* \*

IN INDIA · LESSON # ONE

GOLDEN HANDSHAKE Passing a temple a seedy looking type is all smiles and shoots out a warm handshake; very impolite to refuse, you clasp hands... CAUGHT! A vice grip holds you and quick as you can say 'baksheesh' a religious bracelet is fastened to your wrist. You can pay one rupee or be a boor and tear it off.

Henceforth, near temples, keep your hands in your pockets & nod.

The Black Holes of Calcutta are any city bus there. As many people ride hanging off the outside as ride inside giving the double-deckers a perpetual list. Inside? Imagine a riot in an overbooked sauna.

\* \* \*

The handyman, busboy, water boiler, and clothes washer at the Timber Lodge, Darjeeling, was called Top Quality as that was all he could say in English. He also sold dope, 'top quality'.

The 'hot showers' advertised there were buckets of water heated over a woodfire by Top Quality and slewed over oneself in a draughty dungeon. The residue probably left a ring around the Ganges, and in the winter cold of northern India, left me with a wracking chill.

The 'Tibetan tea' (salt, butter, sugar and tea resins) I had in Kalpokri several days later, left me worse. On the serpentine mountain track into the clouds for Everest views at Sandkphu, I was devastated with cramps, dizziness and vomiting. I had been following a Sherpa family and they descended to aid me. Grandad, with a steel cane to assist his broken leg, offered to carry my pack. His son produced a linty mint for me to suck away the foulness.

For two hours upward the family stuck by me, coaxing and moving at my faltering snail's pace. The kids roamed to pick wildflowers and grandfather sang songs out over cloud-filled valleys. Kanchenjunga though 140 km distant, near Tibet, looked immense and hung eerily white in the

Cop — DIRECTING TRAFFIC
VARANASI

Gandhi

umbrella attached →

Calcutta Traffic Cop

thing at an intersection —
MUZAFFARPUR

61 India

sunlight. In India I was constantly assaulted by the richness of life of the very poor.

The Everest views were fog-bound the next morning, but as always, the travel proved an end in itself. *This* is the distinction between 'traveller' and 'tourist'.

\*    \*    \*

A traveller's diary; Karbita, India/Nepal border.

*A totally sleepless night. I feed ravenous mosquitoes. It occurs to me to set the scene, so I shall:*

*A high-roofed wicker walled box. Corrugated tin for the roof. Dirt, dark and unlittered, for the floor. One bed of hard wooden slats covered by a quilt and a sheet. My hip bones grind against the wood as I roll over. A table at my head holds bottles with candles in them, by which I drew, and a cup of water, which may or may not be boiled. I use it to wash down my malaria tablets in the dark. The bed is a shade short and I bump my head often on the table. My clothes are piled on the dirt beside the bed.*

*Next door are a French couple. On the other side, a family whose kid talks in his sleep. His drunken dad and uncle blather on. Later, the sounds of a dog chasing a donkey, it seems to me, and enraged shouting and running feet. I go outside for a look and step in a mountain of cow shit.*

*Roused at 3.30 for reasons not explained – the bus goes at 4.40. The 'luxury' bus is broken so I get a 10 rupee refund and a half seat on a full local banger. An impossible way to spend 13 hours! But I do, relieved by*

Bikaner, Rajasthan
A SIDEWALK HOT MILK VENDOR ON A GRAND SCALE. HOT MILK, SUGAR & CURD MIXED UP WITH A FLOURISH FOR 75 PAISA (9¢) A GLASSFULL. ENTERTAINMENT FREE.

CHAI (TEA) VENDOR AT ANY RAILWAY STATION

*intervals of lying flat out in the filth of the aisle to sleep. They thought this odd, but the half seat grew unbearable.*

*The trip took 16 hours.*

\*    \*    \*

A world unto itself are the Indian Railways and rare is the locale beyond the eerie floating call of a train whistle in the night.

Queue. Three separate queues to secure one rail booking. If you wish, there are professional place-holders who will queue on your behalf. Each queue culminates with a spindly clerk behind bars who records and cross-references the details of your booking in a half-acre sized ledger that weighs more than he does. Eight days later, and three states distant, your name and berth will assuredly be found on the reservation sheets posted to the side of a coach of the Malawar Mail, Red City Express, or Express Punjab Mail. All the trains have names. The system works, and the booking name need not even be authentic. I was 'Fred Turd' on one occasion.

The train platforms were piled with luggage, mail and the draped mounds of colonies of Indians who live, love, eat, work and play in the station. Out among the steaming locomotives a family of seven, under cardboard, brewed up tea on a small fire fuelled by coal fallen from the engines. Cattle amble aimlessly along the tracks. Porters in dusty red jackets and turbans seem unable to keep awake and bed down among the sleepers.

All train travellers' needs are catered to.

On the Express Punjab Mail—

A middle class couple travelling to Agra unpack a massive mess Kit of lunch and tuck in, throwing the bones on the floor and buying cups of tea from platform vendors. A beggar snakes an arm through the barred window and they fill his bowl, then start their dessert.

Good salt-of-the-earth restaurants (veg and non-veg), 'retirement rooms' (1st and 2nd class, men's and women's) where one can get a billet for the night, waiting and refreshment rooms segregated by class, and lavatories of all persuasions, although for many the tracks seemed to suffice.

The stations are much the same, giving one the uncanny sensation of stepping weary from a train that has gone nowhere.

Conductors are the undisputed Sultans of the Station, and assume a haughty mien. A raise of their hand can throw a 50-coach train into motion, the raison d'etre of this railway universe.

India's locomotives are for the most part gorgeous refugees from the steam era, mammoth, black torpedoes belching haloes of hot cinders and smoke. The engineers and stokers are big jolly chaps in a low-tech world of greasy gears, rods and levers. They brewed tea on the mantel above the boiler gate, and sipped streaked in sweat and coal dust. Scarcely a week went by without newspaper reports of train wrecks in Badcrashabad or Carnageapore or, hopefully, anywhere you weren't.

Trackside, restaurant waiters competed with freelance chefs, hawkers, peddlers and beggars at the carriage windows. All in singsong, they touted their wares – 'A-chai! A-chai!' They saw that no train riders went hungry – or got any sleep at 3 am!

On board you meet a microcosm of India; from lawyers and students in 1st class (discussing politics in what would pass for shocking argument anywhere else) to legless beggars sweeping the aisles of

**MANMAD JUNCTION, WAITING ROOM** — a lousy drawing at a lousy small hour of the morning. I'm tired and furniture was never my forté. My night train to Bombay leaves at 1:00 PM, 3:00 am. or 5:00 (It is, as ever in India, hard to get a strait answer) But I'll make it. Meanwhile it is on with the bad art and the good meal I'm providing for the mosquitoes. They are the only things in the room enjoying themselves. If Van Gogh spent a night in this place for the sake of art he would have cut off both ears ____

3rd class in a whirlwind of dust and litter, collecting a few paise fee before departing on the toe of the conductor's boot.

You can wake up after a semi-comfortable night on the 2nd-class sleeper's drop-down-on-chains plank, and see a completely different India from the one you left at sunset. Plains change to cool uplands, to the seaside, to scorched desert. On the other hand, you might just wake up exactly where you went to sleep, stopped in the middle of nowhere, for no reason.

* * *

Mother Ganges was at low water, and along her banks miles of stairs were being swept. The steps led from the river up to mons-trosities of temples and ghats 600 years past their primes. High-water marks were etched 20 metres up on their crumbling facades. Ladies beat river rocks with washing and butts of the dearly departed smouldered on the burning ghats. Gauntlets of hideously deformed beggars took station on the sidestreets leading to the Ganges. Forehead dot vendors were doing a roaring trade. Bathers, bathwater drinkers, brolly-toting Brahmins, pilgrims, pious in petrified headstands, and naked ash-smeared nutters were drawn to the holy river as a fireball of sun dawned.

This was Benares (Varanasi), 'the City of burning and learning' that the lowest Hindu beggar would give his right arm to die in, if he had one. On the steps, a woman col-lected huge mounds of cow dung from the holy heifers who lounged there, kneaded it

an untouchable sweeping the Temple steps – VARANASI

a pilgrim couple at the banks of the Ganges...

into oversize flapjacks and slapped these up on the temple foundations to dry in their thousands. This may be why she is deemed an 'untouchable'. She smiled and gave me a shitty wave.

\*     \*     \*

Postcard from Kajuraho.
    *Sex temples of Kamdharia Mghedev and Devi are masterworks. Dripping sculpted cupcake monuments to the glories of copulation . . .*
    *There were rats in the toilet of the Raja Inn last night. In Varanasi it was mice. What next? Killer shrews?*

\*     \*     \*

My idea of Hell is doing your dirty laundry under a cold shower to the accompaniment of Indira Gandhi electioneering soundtracks.

\*     \*     \*

I encounter some half-baked rubbish heap in a park; a fellow about four feet nothing, with a hair lip and disfigured face who rides a tiny bicycle. He follows me for a while and we talk of Thomas Hardy, literature, his celibacy and my sex life, which he was confident must be prodigious. He politely begged leave to 'ease himself'. Indians called this 'making nuisance', although you would be tempted to label it 'crapping in the park'.

\*     \*     \*

In and around the Ganges, scores of men of all ages bathing and preening as the sun rises . . .

INDIANS TRYING TO BREAK STONES WITH WET WASHING . . . RANA GHAT - **VARANASI**

VARANASI

THE IRON

Episode in a laundry — fellow takes a mouthful of water and spits it out as a fine mist over your laundry, then he irons this to perfection using a massive two handed hot plate heated over glowing coals.

I got a good look at most of the thief crawling under my bed in Ajmer – he wore a sheet over his head. Slim, dark, and shoeless in brown trousers. This narrowed the suspects down to 300,000,000.

* * *

Christmas morning, and I had the Taj Mahal all to myself at daybreak. This once in a lifetime moment was rendered comic as I had to dance barefoot on the slabs of refrigerated marble that surround the Taj in mid-winter.

* * *

There are 'Towers of Silence' in Nehru Park, Bombay, that I never saw. Cadavers are cleaned by buzzards atop the sacred towers, but a family of beggar-acrobats (Dad lay on his back and tossed his kids around with his feet) on the median strip opposite Chowpatty Beach, and intestinal botulism bombs always diverted my attention.

Oh well. A street mystic who divined my mother's first name with no prompting also predicted that I would return to India twice more. So I suppose I shall see the Towers. I hope so. Of 55 countries visited to the date of this writing, India is my favourite.

* * *

Commit no nuisance
Use Toilet Blocks
Sahid Minor /
at nominal fee. P.W.
CALCUTTA – IN THE MAIDAN
Committing nuisance...

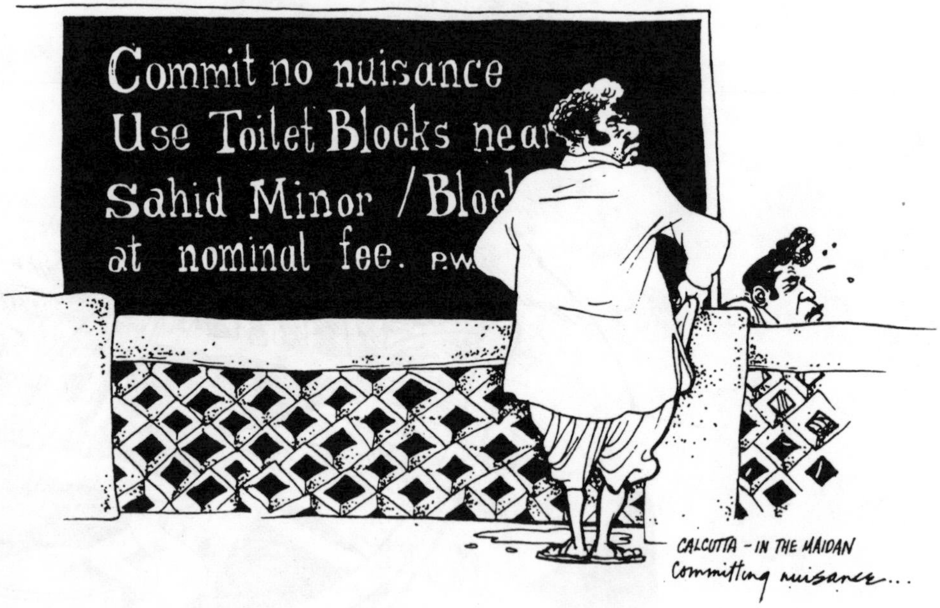

# Nepal

Kathmandu gets to some. It sets them free of convention to indulge any extravagant mood. A Halloween scene.

Durbar Square is *the* place to see and be seen, and I sit up on the temple steps, drawing and drinking it all in, swooping down periodically to tail some particularly bizarre case. The streets are mediaeval pigsties bordered by tiered houses ornamented with erotic fretwork. Idols of the elephant-faced boy glisten with chicken blood – knife provided by the temple. Up the street ('Pig Lane') Eric Clapton blasts out of the 'Chai and Pie'. Kathmandu's pie shops are groovy grottoes dispensing pies, chai (tea), hashish nirvana, and accumulated wisdom from 'the Road'. The Mellow Pie Shop, Om Guest House, Bluebird Cafe, Aunt Jane's, and many others.

Kathmandu is a spaced-out alien spaceship landed in the middle of the 16th-century peasant panorama that is Nepal.

A guest book muse wrote: 'Tourism is more destructive than war'.

\*   \*   \*

Diary entry; Barabise, Nepal.

*Had numerous cups of tea and dahl bread which street vendors are frying up in rings. Started a sketch of the teashop (my 'local', right down at the end of town) and continued this off and on all day while drinking tea there, sitting on a wooden box. During the*

LADY FIELDWORKER

NEPALESE GIRL SEPARATING WHEAT FROM THE CHAFF

WHOMP WHOMP WHOMP WHOMP WHOMP

CLOCKWORKERS • TWO PEASANTS ENERGETICLY FLOGGING A PILE OF WOOL INTO MANAGEABILITY IN UNENDING PRECISION

...And the wildest dreams of Kew

Are the facts in —

# Kathmandu

R. KIPLING —

Hair tinted red, yellow and green

Dropouts, deadbeats
freaks, geeks
poseurs, mutants
& hangers out —

THE SCENE IN DURBAR SQUARE

DAD TRYS HIS WINGS

USA
XXX
GRADE A
FLOUR

....lounging on the temple steps

*late afternoon a child was pulled out of the river, drowned. The distraught father ran through the street with her in his arms.*

\* \* \*

Nepal makes one trek conscious. The guest books and notice boards of traveller haunts are filled ad nauseum with glowing descriptions of newly discovered trekking possibilities. All a bit much. In response I penned 'Trek to room D' in a mountain cafe in Dhulikel. Reports reach me three years later that this was still being quoted. Subsequent trek reports were prefaced with 'quite an interesting trek but nothing compared with the trek to room D', etc.

*The Trek To Room D*
*This is a much overlooked but very pleasurable trek and not nearly as arduous as that to Namobuddha or Panauti. From the restaurant it can be combined with a short trek to the toilet to make a full and interesting day. Is recommended you have good footwear (a sturdy pair of thongs) and perhaps an umbrella or poncho as the weather may take a nasty turn. It is the best to set out before 5 pm so as to be back in plenty of time for dinner.*

*Starting from any table in the restaurant, proceed on the level to the doorway (north wall, fairly centrally located). You may encounter friendly waiters en route who can direct you. Once through the door, the trail leads down the steps to a flat, central courtyard. A side track to the toilet can be made from here, just carry on straight for a*

Tea shop in Barabise - Nepal

short while, the toilets will appear in a line before you. They are clean and fairly recent, but of some interest to stool buffs.

Proceeding onward, keep the clothes line on your left. The route goes up a small steep step and through the door to the central lodge. Those fatigued can find a rest area here and drinking water is near at hand. This may be a good spot to have a light snack and a breather before tackling the steep ascent of the stairs. This climb some find daunting, but press on as a view from the window of room D is something for the privileged to see.

It is seven or eight steps up to the first landing. Drinking water is available also on this stage. The route turns sharply, cutting back across the landing, before rising another eight steps to the rarified air of the second floor. It was on this stage, that the French expeditions of '53 and '55 were lost. The way is much easier now, though there is not yet a banister. From here the way is easy, slightly left across the landing to the door marked 'D'. You've arrived. Go to bed you lazy bastard!

\*   \*   \*

Everest is of course the ultimate trek. Up the Solu and Khumbu valleys through Namche Bazaar, to the 'Roof of the World'.

I started out apprehensive in track shoes and sweater and ended up knee deep in the first snow of the Himalayan winter, guided by a Sherpa, and wearing full down suit, balaclava, snow goggles (astonishing glare!) and hiking boots that my guide

AT NAGARKOT, MT. EVEREST VIEWPOINT, WAITING FOR THE CLOUDS TO CLEAR ...

Sherpa !

THE RENOWNED STRONGMEN OF THE HIGH HIMALAYAS. I ENCOUNTERED MANY IN NORTHERN INDIA EN ROUTE TO HOME VILLAGES, UP TO A WEEKS TREK AWAY ACROSS CHILL VALLEYS, EACH LADEN WITH 50 KG. OF SALT

Yes, barefoot!

Which way to the Mountains Man?

←policeman

SCENE ON New Road - Kathmandu.

assured me had been to the top of Everest with him on the '76 Japanese women's expedition. I made 5545 metres to the top of Kala Pathar, a windswept pimple at the foot of the Everest ice fall. The 'Attic of the World'? The most exhilarating spot I have ever been.

*   *   *

OLD AS THE HILLS

Gentlemen among the Himalayas

# Egypt

It is winter in Cairo, chilly and dismal. In a cafe I take a nice English tea and joust with a steady stream of postcard and sunglass hawkers, souvenir sellers, 'baksheesh' beggars (one constant in a changing travel universe) and a fellow trying to unload German marks. Arab hawkers are the world's worst, bar none! All around me men needing shaves sit drinking sweet tea or tar-like coffees from shot glasses while playing dominoes or dice games. Sawdust on the floor.

The skyline is minarettes. The paved streets are filled with mud, the mud streets are filled with ruts, men in night shirts engulfing the tiny donkeys they ride, and heavily made-up women all in black gnawing sugar cane. The sounds of Egypt: the Muslim call to prayer, being heckled by wheezing donkey laughs. Oranges are cheap, apples exorbitant. Street corner felafel men feed me. Desserts are stomach-sinking slabs of honey-saturated cakes from the pastry shops.

It's travel. You don't always have to be in motion. Every day life goes by and makes you part of it. It makes you glad to be there and forget all the cold showers, tortuous train trips, heart-breaking squalor, bouts of loneliness, illness and doubt. It is me in my Kathmandu sweater and new winter socks (from Omar Effendi's shop) against the chill, weaving through the car horns and crowds of couples on Talat

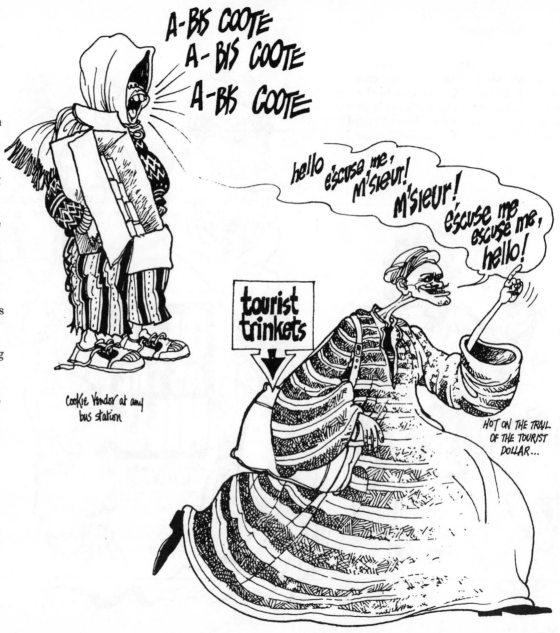

A-BIS COOTE
A-BIS COOTE
A-BIS COOTE

cookie vendor at any bus station

tourist trinkets

hello e'scuse me, M'sieur! M'sieur! e'scuse me, e'scuse me, hello!

HOT ON THE TRAIL OF THE TOURIST DOLLAR...

74

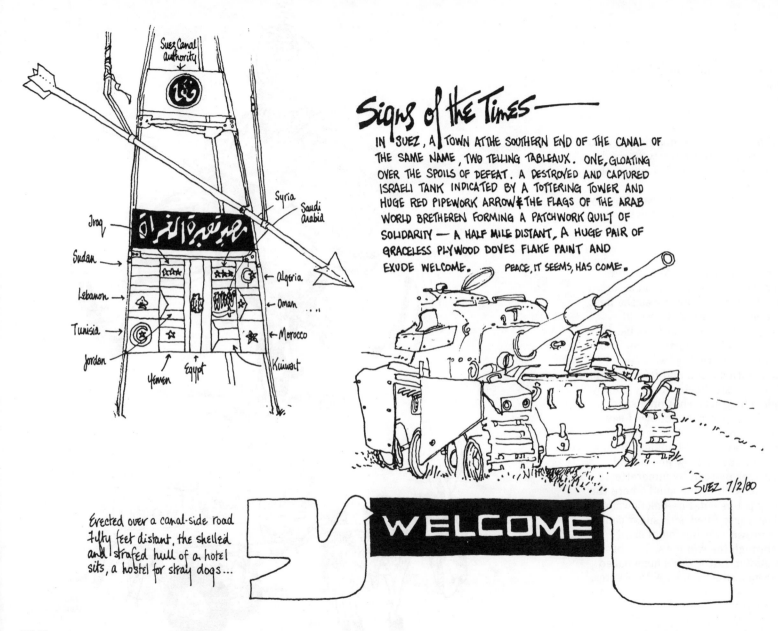

Suez Canal authority

Iraq
Sudan
Lebanon
Tunisia
Jordan
Yemen
Egypt
Syria
Saudi Arabia
Algeria
Oman ...
Morocco
Kuwait

مصر تقدية الحراة

## Signs of the Times—

IN SUEZ, A TOWN AT THE SOUTHERN END OF THE CANAL OF THE SAME NAME, TWO TELLING TABLEAUX. ONE, GLOATING OVER THE SPOILS OF DEFEAT. A DESTROYED AND CAPTURED ISRAELI TANK INDICATED BY A TOTTERING TOWER AND HUGE RED PIPEWORK ARROW & THE FLAGS OF THE ARAB WORLD BRETHEREN FORMING A PATCHWORK QUILT OF SOLIDARITY — A HALF MILE DISTANT, A HUGE PAIR OF GRACELESS PLYWOOD DOVES FLAKE PAINT AND EXUDE WELCOME.          PEACE, IT SEEMS, HAS COME.

— SUEZ 7/2/80

Erected over a canal-side road fifty feet distant, the shelled and strafed hull of a hotel sits, a hostel for stray dogs...

WELCOME

Harb, munching on a take-away felafel and day-dreaming.

\*     \*     \*

The pyramids stand on the margin of Cairo at the abrupt transition from city to sand. They are a monument to the 7-Up can, the litter of preference in Giza.

The film *Cleopatra* was just released – only 15 years late Men grab my ass in the theatre.

\*     \*     \*

Down the Nile by train to Aswan and Luxor to see the burial bunkers and assorted bric-a-brac. A bit disappointing as the best of these are on tour around the world. What's left was just bloody *old*. As usual, the travel surpassed the destination. The 1st class train was a treat; a two-man compartment with air-con and folding sink. Soft berth and clean sheets. A very bumpy ride, though. The tracks shift on a sand base. From the dining car windows I saw two Egypts. On the right, an irrigated green strip, the broad and bankless Blue Nile cut by feluccas; narrow low-walled labyrinth villages pierced by minarettes. To the left, dusty cliffs and sand where the oasis abruptly peters out. Fire-ball dawnings. The 3rd class car is filled with sugar cane butts and a brown swirling fog of sand sucked in through the windows. The best thing about Aswan-Luxor was a huge baked fish dinner from a street vendor – 25 piastres.

\*     \*     \*

A most common sight...

مبيل Mobil

OIL TANKER

Donkeys make frenzied amorous dashes when 'aroused'. They are easily 'aroused'. You get a donkey to stop by twisting his ear as hard as you can.

* * *

'Forbidden!' I detest the arrogant authoritarianism of Egypt. 'Forbidden!' says every loutish boy-soldier with a machine gun, bare-foot in unlaced boots. 'No Entry!' Accommodation was made difficult. Many of the hotels saying 'Complet' although blatantly this was not the case. They just didn't want all the passport-police-immigration cop hassles that foreign guests bring.

Still, I encounter over-whelming kindness, and many strangers who smile and say 'Welcome to . . .' Luxor, Ismalia, Alexandria, or wherever.

* * *

The Red Sea is very, very blue; surreal against the flat tan Sinai on the other side. Dirty mobs of ships are queued up in Suez and pass through the canal in steady sequence. The skyscraper ships pass silently, seemingly splitting the desert. Grand, save for the military nay-sayers who are everywhere with rocket launchers, litter and 'forbiddens!'

* * *

Sanhur, El Fayum Oasis;
   Stone-throwing gangs of kids are an unpleasant phenomenon unique to Egypt.

The Egyptian military often acted like obnoxious boy scouts, heavily armed brats. This fellow was quiet and courteous. He had a shy smile and a machine gun held together with wire. He would make anyone a pleasant P.O.W

← Pretty harmful looking machine gun

EGYPTIAN MILITARY IN DESERT TAN ISSUE.

ALL THESE DUDES OF THE DUNES SEEM TO WEAR UNIFORMS TWO SIZES TOO SMALL

Pests mostly, but some are malicious. One such incident saw me almost hit in the face during a stone blizzard. I zeroed in on the ring-leader and gave chase fully backpack-laden through the dusty labyrinth of Sanhur. The night-shirted brat, screaming in terror, led me a not so merry chase through homes, over roof tops and donkey stables. I was his living nightmare, enraged and breathless, just beyond reach.

He lost me and I was ringed in by agitated villagers. There is not much excitement in Sanhur, not since Tut died. I drew pats on the back and Arab versions of 'There, there now'. And hospitality, an invitation to lunch . . .

A group of 20 men sit around me. I squat on a dirty palm mat in the corner of a single room. My host squats beside me. A small round table is brought out, breakfast remnants still clinging. Lunch is fried fish, breaded tomatoes, a handful of salt flung on the table. The walls are turquoise and on them are painted ships and airplanes in a childish hand. I'm introduced by name to everyone in the room. I tell, in translation, of my travels around Egypt. My hosts are impressed. A tide of women and kids flow through the door to be shooed out occasionally. I have difficulty explaining that I am an artist. I point at the paintings and for a long while they think I am an airline pilot. I tell them of my world of travels and give my host my last clean Canadian flag. He offers me a cigarette and seems shocked a man does not smoke.

They took me by the hand and led me outside. Before I left I took a group photo

Justice done

I'd poked my camera into a hundred places and faces; when a little Arab boy pulled out a cheap plastic camera – fair enough – I gave him a memorable pose. He gave me a squirt. It was a water pistol ————

WELCOME TO SUEZ

EGYPTIANS ARE A FRIENDLY PEOPLE. HANDSHAKES ARE FREQUENT FIRM. VERY FIRM! OFTEN OBJECTS OF AN EXAGGERATED DELIVERY.

of the village. I was *certain* the little rock-throwing bastard was among them, but all the kids looked the same, and the episode had been forgotten.

* * *

cigarette behind one ear

pencil behind other

A waiter appears bearing the requisites of an evenings enjoyment in the café.

IN THE CAFES OF CAIRO WATERPIPES ARE PROVIDED.

# Morocco

'Ali Baba, Ali Baba, you want . . . ' All bearded young travellers in Arab countries get called 'Ali Baba'. Traditionally, only the old and wise wear full beards and then often only white stubble. So I'm Ali Baba. I only expected 40 thieves, but this was Marrakesh.

'Ali Baba! English! You are English? You want hash? Smoke? Heroin? Cocaine? Opium?'

'You want *business?*' as one simply put it, heavily accented with a dark and worldly look. If you are young and in Morocco, this is expected. At times it seems like every kid over five has a pipeline to the French Connection.

I didn't want 'business'. I just wanted to mind my own, to take in the atmosphere. This was the Medina, the market place, of Marrakesh, full of 'businessmen', merchants and hawkers, hustlers, peddlers, beggars, and bums. They fall into step, block my way, smiling and clutching.

'Ali Baba! my frien' my frien' . . . . '

Expensive friends! They want to know all about me, to be my pal. Then they go into their pitch. They get offended when I try to dissuade them or ignore them. I shouldn't do that to a friend. They persist. They curse me for my insults, and they are sincere in this – a hundred times a day!

In the very heart of the maze that is the Medina of Marrakesh I was cornered by one character who had been at my side,

"Ducks and pigs and chickens call,
Animal carpet wall to wall,
American ladies five foot fall
In blue" MARRAKESH EXPRESS
CROSBY STILLS & NASH

Three american ladies, none in blue in an undistinguished car of the above mentioned express. No animals to be seen. Talk ran to the difference between English & Scotch muffins... what happened to romance?

The name is a misnomer — the train is prone to stop periodicly and wait, without explaination for nothing or no one in particular

Marrakesh Express Train — Morocco

talking, for 20 minutes. I hadn't acknowledged him. In the leather tanners' quarters, the 'grotto of a billion flies', I told him to buzz off. No money! He cursed and spat and made less than subtle threats. Here, surrounded by his flies and friends, I believed them. I was scared.

A proud and haughty Berber came to my aid. He was clean and frank and spoke in English of his sincere disgust at the impressions created by 'bad Moroccans'. He was a Berber, a family man, a mechanic, noble in his 50 dirhams a day. He did not want my money. He would show me Marrakesh. I asked 'how much?' He did not *want* my money. He was hurt. He was proud.

He was lying. Ten minutes later in the shop of his brother, where I wouldn't buy, he was twisting my arm, demanding. Vigorously. 'For my small son,' he said. Their uncle who stood nearby beside a wall of ornately crafted and curved Berber knives wasn't disagreeing. I surrendered my pocket change. I wisely kept my cash secure in a money belt under my jeans. He spat and threw the money down and released me. The tour was concluded.

As I left the Medina (quickly) I recalled a saying to the effect 'we are all either hammer or anvil'. There is no golden rule in the Medina, just 'do unto others'. Period. I would be a hammer.

Later that night, I had dinner in the open-air food stalls in the square adjoining the Medina. As I ate, I digested in silence the spiels and curses of the hustlers who crowded around me. My 'friends'. They

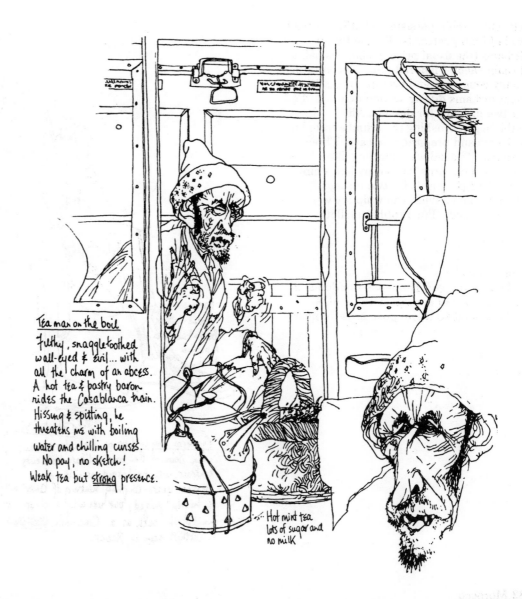

Tea man on the boil
Filthy, snaggletoothed wall-eyed & evil... with all the charm of an abcess.
A hot tea & pastry baron rides the Casablanca train. Hissing & spitting, he threatens me with boiling water and chilling curses.
No pay, no sketch!
Weak tea but strong presence.

Hot mint tea lots of sugar and no milk

left. One urchin persisted, shuffling a thick wad of limp postcards. Twelve for 10 dirhams (the usual price in shops is half a dirham each). I ignored him, concentrating on my cous-cous and carrots. It was 12 for eight dirhams during second helpings, 12 for five dirhams for dessert. Ali Baba began brushing the crumbs from his whiskers and preparing to leave. Three dirhams! The kid was shuffling like a Vegas veteran. The cards flashed by like a movie.

I got 12 postcards for two dirhams. Hammer and anvil! I can whip my weight in eight year-olds! I'm a rubber mallet.

\*　\*　\*

I am a traveller.

'Where you go?' Home via London and my first  too hot shower in 16 months. I would send no travel postcards for nearly three years.

\*　\*　\*

Kareem Abdul-Jabbar Basketball shoes. A muslim touch.

California dreaming...

Moroccan boy-soldiers on leave for holiday week. Down to the bone military hair cuts contrast with haphazard assembly of western gear. Anything hinting of America is highly prized, but usually a cheap imitation such as a Cincinnati BENGALS sweatshirt seen in Rabat.

# Traveller's Truisms

It is illegal in hot countries to drive prudently. You *must* drive *nuts*.

All showers are cold.

Having a cold shower is like hitting your head against the wall. It feels great when you stop.

There is no indignity to which a Third World chicken cannot be subjected.

The capacity for all modes of transport is twice what logic dictates, plus two.

The answer to 'Is this the way to . . . ?' is always 'Yes'. (They're anxious to please and try their English, even if they are wrong.)

Lepers *like* to grab you.

Any country's degree of civilisation can be accurately gauged by the ease of availability of toilet paper.

They cannot change anything bigger than a one.

Always ask to 'see the room'. Vacancies in cheap hotels are always on the top floor. After a long day and a four-flight climb with full pack, the room has to be pretty awful to be refused.

'The Mandi' BATHING IN INDONESIA

toilet

The Mandi is an Indonesian bathroom. To 'shower' one does not hop into the stone basin, one ladles the generally icy water over oneself... an early morning eye-opener.

The universal Malay taxi signal for "Can't stop, pull up." (usually untrue)

At a taxi driver's funeral...
(MALAYSIA)

Roosters don't crow only at day-break.
They crow *any* time you want to sleep.

TV advertising's nuances of laundry powder
spotlessness have no meaning on the road
– 'whiter than white', 'sunshine bright'.
You settle for dingy gray as long as it
doesn't stink.

Freckles are *the* most fascinating entertainment to the dark skinned races of the
earth.

If you can pick up a grape with chopsticks,
you have them mastered.

It's never as bad as people tell you.

It's never dull.

A Combination devoutly to be wished...

hyperactive rooster... + hand grenade....

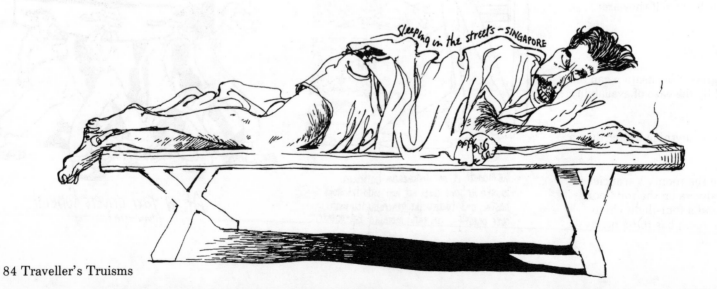

Sleeping in the streets – SINGAPORE

# Africa

## ANATOMY OF A TRAVELLER.

A beat up travel cap is mandatory...

Head full of cultures, currencies & daydreams and destinations...

Why bother shaving?

Trucktop rides give one the windswept ducktail effect.

African jewelry you'd never wear at home...

Those insipient freckles blossom under a tropical sun...

Dress for comfort not style. All faded and mishapen from washing in sinks and hand wringing...

Army shorts have lots of usefull button down pockets. They look better with age...

Tropical bug bite scratching scabs...

The entire Third World wears flip-flops Why tamper with perfection?...

# The Desert

Two and a half years later, back on the Road. My first diary entry: Dakar, Senegal.

*In my first hotel room for 2100 CFA. It's a dump, but I don't know yet if it is an expensive one as the banks won't re-open 'til 3. They are shut over midday after a crack-of-dawn opening. I have only Gabonese CFA so I am really without funds, though taxi drivers assure me they are 'same-same'. I'm lying in my shorts on a battle-field of a bed; sweating, looking at maps and wondering where to go next – but not feeling bad.*

And so begins Africa. With a little paranoia early on – 'Dee-twa, Dee-twa' people say at me in the streets. I take this for 'Detroit' from the front of my T-shirt. I also get called 'Tauba'?

\*   \*   \*

A traveller's room. Bamako, Mali.

*The room is 10 feet by 12 and about 30 deep. The walls are a graduated shade of blue, darkening towards the floor under a stipple of fingerprints, body grime and squashed bug splats. There is a cold-water-only sink, a wobbly chair over which my dirty clothes are draped and an iron bed-stead. The mattress is grimy and curled up at each end like a piece of burnt toast. The sheets match the walls, blue and stained. There is no pillow so I use my rolled-up sleeping bag. Overhead a fan whirls at*

porkpie hat & shades are the norm →

multicolor (all loud) shirt

pastel skin tight trousers necessitate use of a handbag

African touch – a native fly wisk....

TO BE TRENDY IN MALI —

CLACK CLAC-CLAC CLACK CLAC-CLAC CLACK CLAC-CLAC CLACK...

Calabash gourds on a spindle

By the Roadside — MALI

Boys ostracised from their village in pre-manhood rights must fend for themselves. An enterprising troup busk by the roadside in incessant rattling rhythm...

*medium speed, though it is on the highest setting. Its revolutions periodically shake plaster from the moonscape ceiling. It is not too cooling but seems to annoy the mosquitoes, which are small and slow and easy to squash. However, there are a lot of them. The louvred glass window overlooks a dirt courtyard where food vendors sleep, and the floor is red and sticky . . .*

*But nobody bothers me.*

\*   \*   \*

Sitting on the Sahara fringe eating sandy sandwiches and Tunisian oranges, I can't get the Beatles 'Till there was you' out of my brain. 'Birds winging' and 'sweet fragrant meadows' would be misplaced for the next months headed south. I think 'somewhere out there is a scorpion with my name on it . . .'

The orange groves succumb to desert. The highway becomes 'piste', often a kidney-bashing figment of a road passing ragged walled villages anchored to a few palm trees. The piste devolves into a mere direction, a meandering set of tyre tracks in the sand corrugated with ruts and marked by oil drums sand-blasted to bare metal at one km intervals. Hopefully . . . I check out of In Aminas headed for D'janet. If I'm not there in a week they'll send out search parties. Collect! At times the track forks . . . a coin toss. For every vehicle spotted I see two derelict. The terrain alters wildly as does my vocabulary: I am crossing 'regs' – vast gravel plains; then there are 'ergs' like 'The Grand Erg Oriental'

softening goat hides
Gao, MALI

large peanut shaped club

Spinning flax into yarn
–MALI

(some address!) which are full-blown mountain ranges, and 'wadis', erstwhile watercourses full of wildflowers and wildlife.

Few folks turn up but they *all* say 'Ca va?' (How's it going) with gusto. It is the absolute, mandatory first question. I always va 'bien'. Saharan travellers are either gorgeously turbanned and veiled Tuaregs, 'the blue men' or else French or German. The French ride motorbikes and break legs and front forks. The Germans travel in groups all dressed in track suits like soccer goalkeepers. They leave spoors of 'Kaiser Krone', and 'Mund Bier' cans.

It's night, the most beautiful time in Sahara. I sit by a 'guelta' spring in a natural, sand-contoured easy chair with a hot tea against the desert's descending chill. It is spring, the sky is indescribably black and mega-starred and in the uncompeting silence a quiet conversation can be heard for half a mile. I'd tuck in for the night, a circle of flat rock slabs around my head (a Tuareg trick) to keep off sandstorm drifts. It would be cold tonight, cold enough, I hope, to freeze the tails off scorpions.

\* \* \*

The breadshop in Tamanrasset is legend. I've been there and lived to tell the tale.

The bakery opens only when it has bread and it doesn't have bread at any set hour. An expectant horde, all men, formed outside anyway. The doors opened, leastwise one half of the inward swinging double doors did, and a tidal wave of bread buyers

VETERAN.

I BOUGHT BREAD TAMANRASSET

WAITER - Hotel Tahat (POSH) Tamanrasset

surged in. To reach the front counter was literally a battle, Arabs' sandalled feet being their most vulnerable point. Tempers flared. Men sweated, grunted and cursed; few had showered that morning. Nor that month.

The getting in was easier than the getting out. I had reached the counter wanting 15 loaves. Two bakers, surly and dusted in white, served. Battered remnants of baguette bread sticks lay on wooden racks behind them and there was word of a hidden stash under the counter. A very *limited* stash, and those near the front were waving dinars in desperation. 'Quinze!' (Fifteen!) 'Non!' 'Dix!' 'Non!' 'Sept!'

The baker grunted and fired seven still-warm torpedoes across the counter. I had to contort to get hands into my pockets to pay, and clamped the warm faggot of loaves to my chest, the sharp brown ridges atop the bread digging into my arms. But I was pinned, crushed facing the wrong way. I couldn't move and I could barely breathe. I cold-cocked someone with a breadstick to the chin and made a mad, brushing, toe-crushing lunge for the door, head low and elbows pumping like a football back.

I emerged covered in sweat, crumbs, and blood where the ridges had filed into my forearms. I made no friends in that bakery. I made salami and cheese sandwiches instead.

\* \* \*

South of Tamanrasset flies call. Words are exchanged and hostilities declared. War

I AM MISTAKEN FOR A LUMP OF SHIT BY 4000 NEARSIGHTED FLIES....

Tamanrasset, ALGERIA

Windblown hunt for arrowheads... ATOP SAHARAN HAMADA.

Dinnertime for 600 flies
DJANET, ALGERIA

COME N' GET IT!

starts in Fort Laury. This is the shell of an abandoned legion post filled with flies, beer cans and shit. It is on the Michelin map of North Africa because so large a space in the desert without a dot on it would look bad for politicians and map-makers alike.

\* \* \*

In Gazzem takes my grand prize from Port Safaga, Egypt as the definitive Armpit of the Earth. It is a grid of broken-walled huts half drifted over with sand. Ruined trucks are abandoned at random and goats root through the litter. It is horrifically hot and fine, windblown sand coats everything. The Algerian border guards there are in an arrogance competition with their counter-parts across the way in Assamaka, Niger.

How does one conduct 'border formalities' with a gang of informal, boorish, drunken and armed soldiers? With 'cadeaux' (gift-bribes) and fawning courtesy. Don't try to kick a vicious stray dog – 'cruelty to animals is forbidden in Niger! If this is reported you will be sent back!' Sent back to Algeria which you have just left and for which you have no visa, and hence, into the no-man's land between the two countries where you will die among the derelict autos that litter the desert.

A. Henley Smith, a travel companion was moved to write of In Gazzem:

*All the world's a grain of sand,*
*And heaven's in a wild flower;*
*The wind swirls 'round this Goddam land,*

Funeral Band – Nab Robogo, UPPER VOLTA

*And it's getting worse by the hour*

– apologies to Blake

\* \* \*

In Dogon country I am the centre of a minor but memorable cafuffle. I owe the elders of Ir Ily (ear early) a goat.

According to Dogon tribal custom the dear departed are hauled up on ropes and laid in niches in the escarpment beneath which the villages shelter. *Most* of the dead are; some they just pile stones on down in the village. As there tend to be a great many piles of stones, litter, and rubble in these villages, and to the uninitiated one pile looks much like another, I had the misfortune to be found innocently standing atop someone's dead father. This is frowned on. Not the place to be in Ir Ily. Word spread and a gang of greybeard elders gathered, muttering. The muttering rose, orchestrated into a sort of pep rally hate chant. A goat would have to be sacrificed to appease the gods for this abomination. The village was strewn with sacrifical stone pimples over which said goat could be spreadeagled and its throat cut. They wanted 3000 Mali francs to pay for the goat. I apologized. I just didn't have the francs. Somewhere in Mali they have my IOU for one goat.

\* \* \*

Leaving Mali at Kor, I crossed the border of Upper Volta after an hour's drive. The

AFRICA NOTES

The Sahara and Toilet Paper – don't use 2 ply. The desert is windy and it braids in the breeze!

Washing in a Sandstorm.

1. Ignore the soldier, ignore the raven.
2. Hang clothes on convenient barbed wire
3. Tuck towel in belt, hold soap between Knees
4. Stand 2 metres downwind of standpipe
5. Wash out the grease, ignore the sand
6. Blow dry
7. Pretend you are clean

assamaka, NIGER.

disputed no-man's land between the two countries was the usual sunbaked nothingness, an atrocious dust track (Africa was suffering its worst drought in a half century) through a forest of dead, dying and stump trees.

It was not a place of life so I was amazed to meet a tattered scarecrow of a man emerging from the ghostly forest. He had a tiny wizened head and lively, deep-set eyes. He looked rather sad except when smiling, which he did often. He smiled broadly in gratitude when I gave him a peanut butter and jam sandwich and had only two teeth in the upper corner of his mouth, giving his smile an uphill look. He beamed like a child in my company. He spoke no language I could make out, just 'eeehs' and 'aaahs' and delighted, satisfied sounds. I enquired, did he live in Mali or Upper Volta? He didn't understand, but wanted to show me his village. It was noontime and ferociously hot as he led me off through the thorn trees and I had no energy for a hike. I'd been ill with sunstroke in Mopti. So I stopped and shielded my eyes and pretended to see his village off on the heat haze horizon. He was pleased.

He helped me gather firewood to brew up tea and shared this. After lunch I gave him some food and sweets and left him to go off, rags flapping, a man without a country. A Nowhere Man living in his Nowhere Land eager to help anyone for the price of their company.

*   *   *

Mens rest shelter - DOGON VILLAGE, MOPTI

With the appearance of the Nowhere Man came towns and people. Dogondoutchi, Ouahigouya, Biri N'konni and Timbuktu. Timbuktu is just a name, another quiet earth-coloured West African village. It was, however, the hottest place I have ever been. Maybe 115° or 120° F. In the summer they say it is in the 140s.

In Upper Volta the desert was losing its grip. Small villages appeared on the horizon, beehive-shaped mud houses with huge pimple-like grain silos beside each.
As I changed countries the shape of these would change. Bigger towns were sculptured sandcastles, all pink baked mud, bristling with supporting timbers. Mosques are like porcupines.

The people were black now, not Arab, and fantastically dressed. The markets are psychedelic mind-blowers of multi-coloured robes, jewellery, noise and smells. Goods and produce (small and withered and nothing like the riotous abundance of Asia) were arrayed in clusters on the ground and market mannies squatted or lay under reed canopies bartering with shoppers who balanced large half gourd bowls on their heads. It is a pretty capitalism. If I buy I am 'patron'. If I don't I am 'maquereau' (mackerel?)

\* \* \*

Postcard from Ouagadougou (Wog-a-doo-goo), Upper Volta.
*Instead of my usual update, I'll give you a description of this place. I'm sitting in the non-air conditioned dining room (it's cheaper)*

Picture of Innocence

heap of stones

heap of stones

heap of stones

heap of stones

somebody's father's grave.

In Dogon country - MALI

of the Hotel Centrale in Ouagadougou. I'm
sitting down to lunch; a large 'Sovibra' beer
(my second in thirsty succession) and a
torpedo sandwich of 'salade compose' which
is tough and chewy but tasty. They advertise
'hot dogs' here, but you can imagine what
you might find in an Upper Volta hot dog!

The Centrale is kitty-corner to the Grand
Marchee (big market) which is now, at 1.20
winding down for a heat-of-the-day nap. I've
been sweltering my way around the marchee
bartering for blankets – gloriously gaudy
patchwork ones. After much legwork, I
bought two. Much tongue-work too! I haggled
the two down to 16,000 CFA after a kickoff
price of 28,000. Now I'm beat. A sewing
machine man is supposed to have the little
flag patches I ordered ready by three. Last I
looked he was doing a lousy job, so I may
have to hassle about them. I'll have to wake
him up first.

*    *    *

The word is out about the curfew in
Ouagadougou. There *is* one. If you are on
the street after 1 am, they shoot you.

*    *    *

BOUREM, MALI

TIMBUCTOO, MALI

# The Jungle

My Africa greened in Togo. No more endless desert vistas. The horizons became delineated in shades of emerald, the sky a deep rich blue. The road was soft and ran through fathomless forests of green, except for the occasional scarlet of a flame tree.

Villages punctuated the greenery; mud and wattle houses with the compound swept to bare earth and families squatting around fires or under shelters up front. Goats and daredevil kids on the roads. Kids *everywhere*. The roads were red earth and well maintained, the only complaint being with the rain barrier men, who are very quick to put down their gats in seeming anticipation of rain. Power. Truck drivers argued in the roadway in pantomime with these fellows until intimidated by the collective wrath and the queues of gassy trucks urging action. The surrounding forest was vandalized by slash and burn clearing in anticipation of planting in the rainy season (that would not come that year, nor the next).

Checkpoints of officialdom impeded progress; greens and browns. The browns are police. They check on the army, and vice versa. In every cafe and shop a picture of the country's current colonel-ruler was displayed. It would be the same throughout black Africa, and woe betide he who didn't keep abreast of that week's coup.

* * *

Togolese gendarme

anything possible !!!

.... in the jungle grass - Togo.

Capital city of Togo, Lomè is a 'free port' on the Gulf of Guinea and a mecca of western goods and indulgences. Or over-indulgences. After weeks of desert deprivations I pigged out on pizza, steaks, ice cream and beer. While sitting outside the central police station awaiting movement of the wheels of visa bureaucracy my body rebelled.

I felt the call – *the shriek!* – of nature. Across the road a derelict train yard seemed as inviting a lavatory as any in my urgency. There was no real cover and the yard seemed suddenly full of Africans – some making their homes in the disused boxcars. Committed and in desperation I squatted in the fluted stalls of a baobab tree-trunk. The locals are greatly amused. I hunched, wracked by cramps, while they roared for an encore. Pants to my knees I am about to oblige when frantic waving from the building across the street catches my eye.

Upping pants, I hobbled hurriedly over. They bade me enter; 'Vite! Vite!' (Hurry! Hurry!) was my courteous reply. I could barely follow my Samaritans on a jackrabbit run through twisting corridors. They were laughing and I, barely hanging on. A key turned on some bureaucratic privvy. The relief, enormous. Sprawled pooped on their pot, I was already an office anecdote.

Descending the front steps a small crowd cheered and I acknowledged with a sweaty smile and wan wave as if I had just finished laying a ceremonial cornerstone. We were at the Ministere des Affaires Etranges. A strange affair indeed.

\*   \*   \*

Very popular print fabric bearing the likeness of new President Paul Biya. These are seen worn by men and women throughout Cameroon.

Waitress - Yaounde.

Good afternoon sirs. Would you be taking any buns?

Bun Vendor - CAMEROON

Benin is so narrow it can be crossed in an hour or so. Marxist, machine gun-toting soldiers abound, but they are smiling and friendly and it seems a nice, green place.

\*   \*   \*

The border with Nigeria looked a nightmarish train wreck of litter, loiterers, vendors, half-dismantled trucks and buses, mud bogs and obnoxious officials. I made bets with fellow travellers on how long they would detain us. Three and a half hours.

Lagos is almost universally described as a 'hellhole' and the most expensive city on earth. It is. Destitution, prostitution, gangs and gangsterism, freeways choked with anger, appalling pollution, aggression and fear. It has 'an energetic rhythm' said the tourist brochure.

From Lagos' *Weekend Eagle* newspaper:
   *. . . even more nauseating is the role of the night soil men who display mammoth containers overflowing with human intestinal precipitations at conspicuous road junctions. The wonder of it all is that such unsightly exhibitions no longer repulse Nigerians. We are at ease with filth.*

This, a shocking contrast from Ganvie in Benin; a picturesque fishing village out in the ocean entirely on stilts. It was patrolled by a cheery armada of bosomy women in dugout canoes looking like fat brown peas in pods.

The carnage of Nigeria's excellent highways cannot be overstated. Horrific, twisted

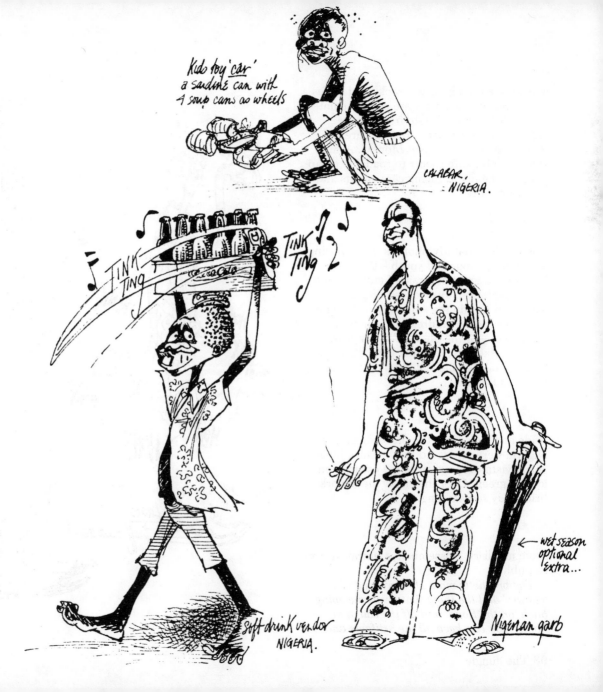

Kids toy 'car' a sardine can with 4 soup cans as wheels

CALABAR, NIGERIA.

TINK TING   TINK TING

soft drink vendor NIGERIA.

← wet season optional 'extra'...

Nigerian garb

wrecks are seen hourly. Trucks and buses pass three abreast. They are gaudily painted and bear legends – 'Help from Above', 'The World is a Stage', 'Blessed are the Peacemakers', 'God, Not Money'. Armed soldiers offer safe escort to roadside campsites. In the night, racing cars, sirens and distant gunfire.

\* \* \*

Eastern Nigeria. My photo is taken posing with a burly, muscled youth – the norm here. It is a great contrast of cultures and of pigmentation. Just myself and a fellow who lived beside the Aba to Ikot Ekpene road. He had no 'address' to which I could send a copy of the photo. Fifteen years ago, it strikes me, he must have been one of the swollen-bellied children of the tragedy that was Biafara.

\* \* \*

Rude and tedious border proceedings exiting Nigeria were mitigated by the stark jungle-shack vista over a river gorge escarpment iced in green. Over the shaky metalwork bridge lay *serious* jungle.

\* \* \*

From my diary: Bossembele, Central African Republic.
*The brochette man. He's my type of 'culture' and the thing that keeps me going back 'on the Road' and off the couch at home. You can keep all the artifacts and*

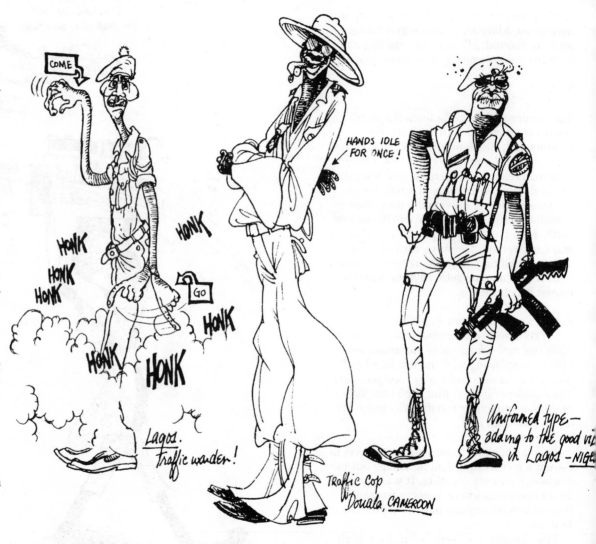

COME

HONK
HONK
HONK
HONK
HONK
HONK
HONK
GO
HONK

Lagos.
Traffic warden!

HANDS IDLE FOR ONCE!

Traffic Cop
Douala, CAMEROON

Uniformed type –
adding to the good vi[..]
in Lagos - NIG[..]

quaint travelogues and textbooks and museums. (I take perverse pride in never going inside museums to study local icons.) Give me the popular icons like the street corner brochette man – a chap selling kebabs of roasted meat done over oil drum fires. Everywhere in Central Africa. One orders up by the brochette, two or three, or more per sandwich at 50 CFA per. To these on a French stick, halved, he adds a grease-curry sauce, sliced onions and perhaps (if I am feeling gluttonous) a peanut oil fried omelette. The quality of the meat can vary, but that too is culture. They can be indescribably delicious.

I am eternally curious and insatiable for these seeming trifles of street life that add up to a culture. They are for me, the reason for travel. Each to his own. I've made little pieces of this world mine – and memories – through this trifling.

Fed a pig at dinner. Macaroni. I didn't much fancy the stuff but the pig took to it and grunted his approval. No big deal, but it is not something I would do at home.

\*　　\*　　\*

The greenery became claustrophobic. 'It's a jungle out there.' Days dawned almost prehistorically. Mists surrounded oversize foliage dappled with sunlight screened through the canopy of leaves 30 metres above. Strata of vines, ferns, mosses, creepers and tendrils competed for the light. The jungle floor spongy with decay. Nothing sharp or harsh except the shrieks of birds and monkeys, echoed and answered.

## Whodunit?

An al-fresco inquisition seeking sorcery in Zaire. The village sorcerer questions implicated parties. The chiefs' wife has died (of evil spirits). He repeatedly examines their palms and measures the breadth of their sholder blades. He finds both innocent and proclaims such in a theatrical judgement punctuated by bongo flurries. The chiefs' brother-in-law done it....

Everything dripped with dew and hothouse life. A tyrannosaur would not have seemed amiss.

The buglife was astounding. Everything oversize. New creepy-crawly horrors of one night became commonplace the next. I have only one rule – 'Don't touch me'. They can come and go as they please, but to crawl on me means instant squashing. A harsh law, but I am outnumbered seven billion to one.

I stripped to orange track shorts for the duration – impeccably dressed to move among the upper crust of blowdart society, who call me 'Barbe'. Bearded one.

One bedtime throbbing drums called to me. I left my sleeping bag for a walk along the eerie moonlit jungle road, coming upon a shouting, jumping mass beneath a huge tree. A whole village, all ages, was turned out on the swept-earth common before their houses. A bamboo easy chair was fetched for me as the dancing continued all around. The activity has no form; the music no orthodox rhythm. No dance with steps, or tune you could hum. All spirit and no form. The drummers pounded incessantly, each in his own tempo. Dancers, mostly women and children did their own thing with much hip action. Some took the lead in the centre of the circle while the others orbited in jogstep. Men made answering chants to the lead singer. An oldster ( I could only make out a grizzled silhouette) did a stiff and abridged version of dance, swaying and making spear-like threats with his walking stick. They were celebrating nothing more than Saturday evening enter-

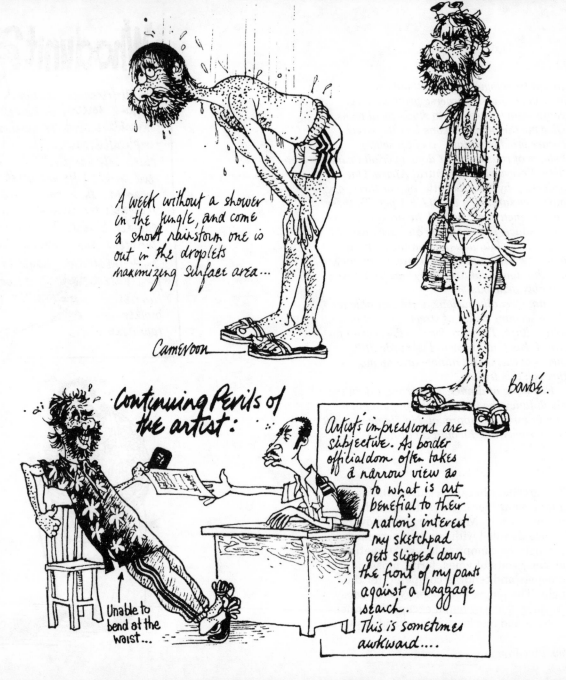

A week without a shower in the jungle, and come a short rainstorm one is out in the droplets maximizing surface area...

Cameroon

Barbé.

Continuing Perils of the artist:

Unable to bend at the waist...

Artist's impressions are subjective. As border officialdom often takes a narrow view as to what is art benefial to their nation's interest my sketchpad gets slipped down the front of my pants against a baggage search.
This is sometimes awkward....

tainment for one and all – teens didn't have to go out and get drunk and crash the family car. Parents didn't have to get away from kids. Kids didn't have to go to bed early.

* * *

Diary excerpt: Bangui, CAR.

Hiked down to the riverside munching a tough brochette. Saw no hippos, only punks blackmarketing Zaires (Zaire currency) in the street. Real or counterfeit? Zaire is in view across the river at Zongo. Whores in the Hotel Roc are friendly and armed with algebra exams as their proof of schoolgirl status.

I'm sitting down by the Ubangi watching little boys fishing from the reeds. The tug 'Bangassou' shunts log barges. The river is wide and streaked with sandbars. Zaire is on the other side. Dugout ladies glide along bending over short pointed paddles. Foodstall life (and me) atop the bank.

Suddenly the dugout ladies bolt, churning for open water. A police boat with three cops rides herd on them and rounds them up, virtually bulldogging away their paddles, leaving them drifting. The whole operation takes five minutes and a forlorn armada of ladies paddle back across the river using hands or buckets.

The cops then parallel the shoreline splashing water with the confiscated paddles into the riverside weeds, flushing out a contingent of squawking women on foot. They filter into the watching crowd and disappear up sidestreets.

Many people with withered limbs are about. They get about levering with a staff.

Alindao, C.A.R.

all the camouflage gear still doesn't disguise a naked power-tripper.

Bambari C.A.R

Bruce Lee imitator C.A.R and everywhere

flattened oil tin

wheelbarrow? C.A.R

*Explanation? A customs raid. The Zaire canoes had come over to blackmarket with the ladies in the reeds. In Zaire they don't have anything. Now they don't have oars either.*

\* \* \*

Traffic was rare now. Mostly beer and soft drink trucks. The people are subsistence-sufficient otherwise. Dark, muscled men popped from the undergrowth like shooting gallery figures. Kids in electric blue school uniform tatters screamed and waved. On the road, centipede invasions and battered bicycles with murdered monkeys lashed to the handlebars.

I entered Zaire bearing visa and obligatory letter from the Canadian embassy saying I'm a great guy. Darkest Africa. At customs I'm frisked and my gear ransacked. They get a pack of cards 'gift' and sell me blackmarket currency out back at a crummy rate. I don't argue.

The road became a set of ruts and muddy cambers through a tunnel of green. I got regularly welted in the head by branches intruding through the truck window; toiled as a roadwork coolie – chopping fallen trees, machete hacking through toppled bamboo, shoring up rotting bridges. Messy blisters festered and scratches and bites wouldn't heal. I thought of Hemingway's *The Snows of Kilimanjaro* in which the he-man hero dies from a thorn scratch gone septic.

Great muddy rivers filled with 'bilharzia', a nervous-system destroying parasite,

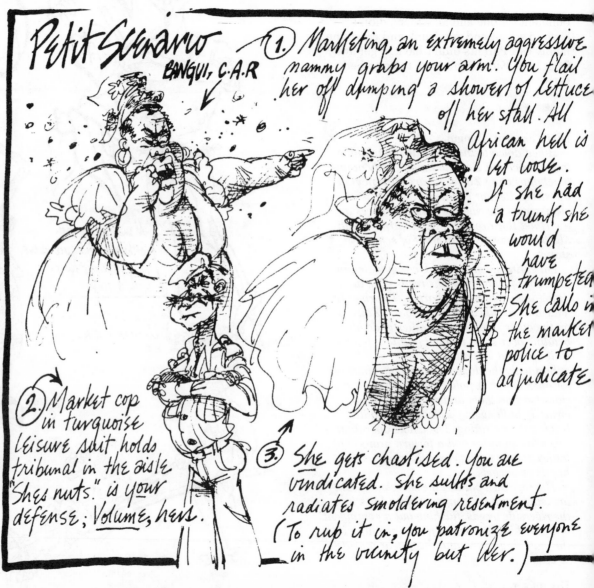

**Petit Scenario**
BANGUI, C.A.R

1. Marketing, an extremely aggressive mammy grabs your arm. You flail her off dumping a shower of lettuce off her stall. All African hell is let loose. If she had a trunk she would have trumpeted. She calls in the market police to adjudicate

2. Market cop in turquoise leisure suit holds tribunal in the aisle "She's nuts." is your defense; Volume, hers.

3. She gets chastised. You are vindicated. She sulks and radiates smoldering resentment. (To rub it in, you patronize everyone in the vicinity but her.)

had to be crossed. Hiring a dugout to ferry me across for the price of a pair of underwear I was untroubled by the muddy mess inside. The mud was caulking. *Bad* caulking and the canoe leaked bilharzia. I may have been hyper-cautious about the waters of Africa, but my nervous system is just fine, thanks. River barges were safer, if they didn't capsize, which looked very possible.

*Bilharzia Blues . . . .*
*I got the bil-har-zia blues ma,*
*Please keep them droplets off of me;*
*Got them old bilharzia blues ma,*
*Parasites you cannot see;*
*You step into the water,*
*You just shook hands with Mr. D.*

The people were dark here, primitive jungley creatures. And poor; they would gratefully accept empty bottles and cans, string, nails, anything. A stalk of bananas for a T-shirt. Contact with these jungle people was edifying. Walking along the green tube of road, you could see necks craning toward your one man parade. A smile or a nod set them beaming. A 'bonjour' started animated chatter that carried to the next shoal of quizzical faces.

The pygmies, tiny and caramel-coloured took me hunting. They beat the jungle trying to drive small game into a quarter mile arc of curtain net. No luck, so we had honeycomb from a wasp's nest. They stunned the stingers with smoke from a huge cigar they purpose-made on the spot.

*   *   *

Bill Harzia

Mal Ana

AWKWARD MOMENTS...

little toe in capfull of Spanish Brandy

ROUTING AFRICAN HOOKWORM

These tiny parasitic sods lurk in jungle mud then burrow into the skin headfirst. Difficult to remove but alcohol is said to be of use...

In the clear highland air of Uganda, where there are 'troubles' (a civil war), I froze in my sleeping bag 16 km from the equator. Southern Uganda is Switzerland with bananas. The Rewenzori mountains – the 'Mountains of the Moon' – recede as rolling hills and mist-filled valleys like a Mona Lisa backdrop. Cattle herds, cyprus-lined roadways and picturesque ladies in the 'Nepal crouch' under loads of firewood. Picnic land . . . 'until the shooting starts'.

I got my first greeting in Swahili. 'Jambo!'

*   *   *

Market mango
lady's liturgy—

Yaounde
CAMEROON

# The Savanna

To the east of the green overlay on the Michelin map of Central Africa lay the great savannas where I am 'mzunga' – white man, or 'bwana' – Lord.

In Tanzania, even we Lords go short. 'Yes, we have no bananas' is the national anthem. There were no brochette men there; nor any bread or the flour to make it with. No cooking oil, toilet paper or milk powder. There was even a shortage of Tanzanian flags – these were being held up at the port of Dar Es Salaam, or maybe in Holland where they are all made. The pleasant Indians who operate Tanzania's empty shops have perfected the resigned smile. 'You'll learn', they said and rationed themselves to another blackmarketed cigarette. There were none in the shops. There was petrol rationing and unruly queues at the stations. Never were there line-ups at the bookstores to read the ubiquitous political tracts of President Julius Nyerere, the 'brains' behind the operation. But his official portrait in all the shops pictured him as a smiling grandad, and this was a nice change from the stern military gorilla types leading most of Africa.

Tanzania is essentially a zoo without a snack bar; one vast game park. Headliners are the 'Big Five' – lion, hippo, rhino, giraffe and elephant. The supporting cast is lead by the warthog, the ugliest thing on earth next to an enraged racist. It is tse-tse fly territory and, as I don't have a tail, I

etiquette in the savanna

Never prefer a handshake to African children whilst standing in a cow pie. However well intentioned, it creates a flippant impression...

— TANZANIA

105

murdered hundreds of them with a copy of *Lord Jim*.

The Serengeti is an immense grassland roamed by nomadic herds and the predators who stalk them. Its silence is awesome and lit by that peculiar golden East African glow. Nights are a little different.

A truck bog-down necessitated an overnight bivouac out in the untamed centre of the Serengeti. This is the stuff that ends up as an eyebrow raising column in the Nairobi newspapers – 'Tourists devoured by lions'. I camped close to a huge fire, my tent-peg mallet inside my sleeping bag and a carved wooden lion idol (from Nigeria) standing guard outside. Fearful of him being abducted by marauding baboons I later brought him inside the tent too. Grunts are heard nearby in the night, and the rising cries of hyena. I dream of myself running with one clamped to my lips while the pack rips out and devours my intestines. (This is hyena 'modus operandi'.) And of my bones bleaching by some salt lake, ringed by a million pink flamingos. Africa, where men are men, except when they are *dinner*.

\* \* \*

I am watching the interplay of a kill. In Ngorongoro Crater, a lioness leisurely pulls yards of guts from the fresh-killed carcass of a wildebeest. Powerful indolence. A small, skittish jackal moves on the periphery in exaggerated slow-motion caution, anticipating a snack. When the lioness moves off a few paces for a drink and a shady

*In the game parks one can get easily spooked...*

siesta he rushes in, all paranoid energy, bloodying his snout and gulping mouthfuls between panicked glances. Ma lion gallops back snarling, driving him off. The procedure is repeated several times until she falls on the carcass in utter disdain and goes to sleep.

*   *   *

Near Nairobi there is a *line* down the middle of the road. Civilisation! I had my jungle boots excavated of mud and polished by the shoeshine men on Kenyatta Avenue. My clothes, soaked in the bathtub, left a quagmire of filth. Poste Restante brought folksy news from home, and newspaper clippings of African atrocities. Upper Volta is now Bourkina-Faso. A family of French tourists were killed in coup crossfire.

Nairobi's traveller, tourist and poseur node is the Thorn Tree Cafe of the New Stanley Hotel. One sips tea, trades tall tales and leaves messages on the cafe's shady thorn tree. Landrovers among the skyscrapers. Four hours up the nearby Uhuru Highway, within the walls of the Great Rift Valley lie tribal grazing lands. These people were delighted to be sketched, and could readily identify rival tribespeople from my drawings – Bokot, Masai, Samburu. Wildly two-tone painted men with spears followed their herds. Their women were ringed, tassled, banded and bejewelled beyond all bounds.

Beyond the bounds of Muslim propriety the Kenyan Rail Service would not let me

→ MY SAMOSAS.

Waiter, New Star Cafe LAMU.

Staff at MONTY'S TAKE AWAY Muindi Mbingo Rd.

Typically Kenyan, friendly, hardworkers and GENUINE... good SAMOSAS too...

and some travel companions go. Men and women are not allowed to share the same train compartment to 'the Coast' – Mombassa and Kenya's exotic Arab sea coast despite the fact that every hotel in Mombassa is a brothel. The womenfolk cloistered, we men retired to the train's 3rd class bar and drank 'Tuskers' with the locals, who smoked and sweated and called me 'father'.

Lamu Island is as Arab as East Africa can be. It was epitomized by 'Boris Karloff' my habitual waiter at the New Star Cafe on the island's main lane. He fetched honey yogurts with disdain, wore a scowl, and a misshappen white star on his tattered blue jacket. His face was scarred by knives. He is of the dusty Muslim backstreets of this whitewashed isle. The crumbling-facaded lanes are choked with travellers in native regalia, Arab women the size of galleons in black bags, manacled prisoners in pajamas, and nightshirted men driving donkey carts. My request for John Lennon's 'Cold Turkey' on the tape deck is overruled by the Muslim sunset call to prayer blaring from Lamu's mosques. Boris Karloff goes to his knees and faces Mecca. East meets west on Lamu.

\* \* \*

A traveller's diary

*. . . Cabs to Marangu, Tanzania leave from the Esso station on the Haile Salassie end of River Rd, Nairobi. I am shoehorned into a battered taxi in the middle rank of four adults and a lap-sitting child. Beside*

Bored Indian – NORFOLK HOTEL BAR    Nairobi

Colonial Legacy
Lord Delamere Terrace – NORFOLK HOTEL    – Nairobi

me is Dave (with whom I would travel for half a year) and a Masai youth in full regalia. A family of five Indians sit in back. The lot is prowled by moneychangers black-marketing – their left socks are stuffed with foreign exchange, their right ones are vaults for Tanzanian currency folded in bundles of ten 100-schilling notes. I get 50 to the US dollar. Official rate in Tanzania is 12 something.

We approach the border with the best of intentions, underwear full of illegal currency, sketchpads (they don't need any reason to confiscate anything) and taboo South African-visa passport. There is barely room in there for me!

The tatty blizzard of telexes at Tanzanian immigration does not yield our required 'permission to enter' from Dar Es Salaam's chief of police (in response to our official request, telexed six weeks earlier). Good-bye Tanzania . . . Thinking fast, Dave goes to check the telex carbon copies at nearby police headquarters. He carbon-forges our names in addendum to another party's permission. Police accept this and contact immigration. A sweaty moment when they go to recheck the originals, but I've been fore-warned and have torn this unaltered one out. On the strength of the carbon forgery and ingratiating palaver we are admitted.

Leaving immigration, I slip back the purloined original. 'May and R. A. Dennis' need not thank us. We are devious but not without scruples.

The border taxi bump-starts toward Arusha. Masai riders are fascinated with beards and stroke our hairy arms like kittens.

I admire their beadwork and offer a pair of cutoffs in exchange. They want the shorts as a gift and sulk in odiferous silence when no deal is struck.

We are checked at *four* police roadblocks. An Indian lady has her trunk marked 'pots', roughly gone through each time without complaint from her, or a courteous word from the officials. She has plastic tea trays, tin pots and cutlery, coathangers, shabby bundles of clothes and a pack of broken biscuits. I itemized them as she laid them out on the roadside.

In Arusha we hole up at the Corner Hotel. It *is* on a corner and a dump. We are lucky to get it. There is a National Bank of Commerce regional managers conference in town and all the hotels are full. We dine 'downtown' by the clock tower, eating street stall grub wrapped in newspapers full of Marxist anti-US rhetoric of the most blatant sort. Post dinner beers are taken at the New Arusha Hotel lounge. The waiters serve with conspiratorial asides about black-marketing and appear saddened when we dismiss them as possible government provocateurs. The lounge patrons are jolly drunken men in pale 'Nyerere' leisure suits. They apologise for the appalling shortage of everything in Tanzania but friendliness. They are, as it turns out, the convening bank managers on an off hour. Should I put myself foreward as tomorrow's guest lecturer on 'economic sabotage' (black-marketeering)?..

\* \* \*

SO IM AN 'ECONOMIC SABOTEUR'.... A LOWLIFE DEALER IN THE BLACKMARKET. EVIL? IMMORAL? BUT WHO'S BEING HURT? THE OFFICIAL EXCHANGE RATE IS LUDICROUS. THEY'RE SCREWING THE TOURIST! THE WHOLE ECONOMY OPERATES ON THE BLACKMARKET — IT HAS TO 'CAUSE THE GOVERNMENT CAN'T PROVIDE EVEN BASIC NECESSITIES.... IM 'SABOTAGING' AN UNWORKING AND UNREAL SYSTEM. WHY SHOULD MY BUCKS FINANCE AND PERPETUATE THEIR STUPIDITY?

... ON THE OTHER HAND IM BRINGING VALUABLE FOREIGN EXCHANGE TO THE MAN IN THE STREET, WHERE ITS REALLY NEEDED! IM A REALIST, A PRAGMATIST, HELPING THE MASSES TO COPE. A FREEDOM FIGHTER !!....

WHAT THE HELL, ILL HAVE THE HUNDRED AND FIFTY SCHILLING STEAK.... BLACK MARKET ITS ONLY 3 BUCKS!

Moral Dilema Resolved....
MOSHI TO DAR ES SALAAM NIGHT TRAIN

On Zanzibar island, now formally part of Tanzania, separate, punishing, currency arrangements from the mainland are nonetheless required. Dave proffered a business card taken from the American embassy in Dar Es Salaam identifying him as the US second vice-consul. I was his aide. As 'resident aliens' we were exempt from this monetary con-job.

\*   \*   \*

'As wide as all the world, great, high, and unbelievably white in the sun was the square top of Kilimanjaro.'
    Ernest Hemingway – *The Snows of Kilimanjaro*

With a guide and two porters carrying my food and tackle I reached 4650 metres on Mt Kilimanjaro. This, after three days through thick rainforest, fire-scorched scrubland, and frigid, high altitude tundra. But not through High Altitude Sickness, the only cure for which is descent. I'll never see Africa from atop its high peak.

\*   \*   \*

Dar Es Salaam means 'haven of peace'. It isn't. I buy a knob-kerrie – a sort of sceptre, an ornamental skull crusher favoured by the tribal chiefs and elders of East Africa – and parade the unlit streets at night, twirling and brandishing it like a menacing drum-major.

\*   \*   \*

111 The Savanna

No problems entering Malawi. They gave my backpack a going over, dwelling particularly on the reading matter. *Lady Chatterly's Lover* drew some attention, but I knew what they were looking for, I'd been forewarned. They were looking to sieze copies of *Africa On the Cheap*. It had nasty truths to tell about their President Banda. I had it stuffed down my pants.

\* \* \*

Note from my diary

*. . . Malawi has things, and at reasonable prices. No blackmarket as a result. Will have to go back to honesty, 'cold-turkey'.*

\* \* \*

Nakonde, Zambia is pretty much a one-horse town. A smuggler's horse. It is just a stroll from Tanzania and the smuggling is blatant, although someone gets shot every so often as a reminder.

Dave and I were warned not to walk down the Nakonde-Chitipa (Malawi) road or ' . . . you will be beaten, or more bad, you will be killed'. The road, in addition to intermittent bus service, seemed to feature thieves and murderers. The Zambians say they are Tanzanians. The Tanzanians blame Zambians.

Our eventual lift was with an Indian 'commercial traveller' (smuggler?) in an armoured panel van. He had a complement of paid riders up front so we climbed in back at 15 kwacha for two (haggled down

Waiter. NAAZ CAFE, DAR ES SALAAM

Arrogant Little Cop
- DAR.

from 10 a piece.) The ride was rolling Hell!
Three hours in the back of a windowless –
they were welded shut against thieves – tin
cell, sucking choking dust and spine jarring
bumps, and living with the very real danger
of overturning in a ditch. Next time give
me the thieves and murderers.

\* \* \*

In the nameless Nkata Bay restaurant – a
dark pit lit by candle stubs – a cheery,
little, hunched dwarf lady served me a huge
meal of rice, omelette, tea and curried
'chambo' from the lake. I glistened with
sweat. All around me sat the shadowy
shapes of fishermen grasping steaming
balls of *msima* in the gloom and transistor
static. Msima is the East African staple; a
huge rubbery blister of congealed maize-
flour dough. I never developed a taste for
it but often considered using the stuff to
cushion my backside from the punishment
dealt by north Malawi's tortuous roads.

Dave and I shared truck rides with
locals, live pigs and birds tied to sticks,
sitting atop heaps of goods piled onto the
battleship-sized flatbed trucks. Windburn,
sunburn, heartburn from quick cafe stops,
police checks.

I saw Lake Malawi in slit-trench dugouts,
filled with fish for ballast. No 'Bilharzia
Blues'; this lake is pure and filled with
tropical fish. And 'aquatic panthers' according
to a wild Zimbabwian army deserter full of
'chambo' (fish) and 'chamba' (dope).

\* \* \*

Restauranteur at his shrine... 'The Spike'

I'M STUCK!!

ONE RIDES **ON**, NOT **IN** A LAKE MALAWI DUGOUT CANOE...

From my diary:

*. . . Met a man on the truck today. Former miner in Zambia. Said he was now.. 'Playing with Mr Hoe. Not much money at the end of the month, only eating'. He farms.*

\*   \*   \*

Malawi civilizes toward the south. Blantyre is a little bit of Britain. The day of my arrival, the Blantyre Sports and Cricket Club presented its 'Bad Taste Disco'. I considered going as is.

I bade goodbye to Dave, had the tailor men on the street by the 'riverfront' mend my tatty kit, and bought an air ticket to South Africa. I left recalling the words of the editor of Malawi's National News Service. His *Daily Times* newspaper had called me Mr Jerkins (Friendliness touches Canadian Cartoonist) and fabricated propagandic quotes, but he had told me ' . . . Travel is like dancing. You are not careful, or sure to place every step, but you can just move as the spirit takes you'.

\*   \*   \*

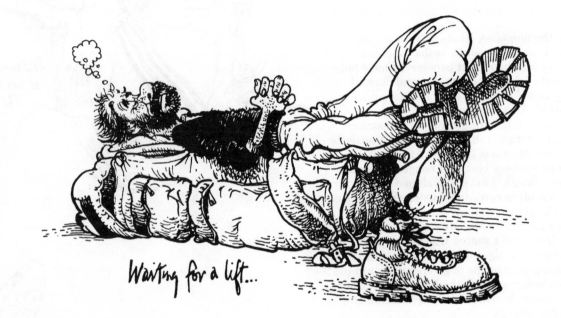

Waiting for a lift...

# The South

I miss Africa. I left it by the roadside somewhere south of Monkey Bay. I'm in 'South'; the Republic of South Africa, and on a formal basis with the Republic as I was obliged to leave a 1200 Rand deposit with immigration at Jan Smutts airport against my failure to depart. The price of respectability. 'Bum' insurance.

Getting around South Africa, however vast, there is no getting away from the question of race. Hitching lifts from criminally reckless drivers (despite driving European supercars over the perfect roads that web the veldt South Africa has the highest auto fatality rate on earth), we regularly have near misses with blacks dashing from the verge – a phenomenon throughout Africa. There is increasing evidence in South African society of blacks outstanding in their field, but on a Sunday afternoon you're more likely to encounter blacks out standing in the road, pickled on pulpy home-brew beer.

I rent a car and give a little black boy in gorgeous pastel school togs a lift. He climbs in *the back*, as he must, it's the law. Departing, he says 'Thank you, master'. Nearly every black hitcher I pick up smells of unwash or booze; about half of them ask for money on exit. Sad. A strange broken black man calling himself 'Mosquito' laments his obvious wounds – scabs, scars and a broken arm in a belt sling. He had jumped from a TV antenna in Botswana when he

— Entering 'South' —

Hitching lifts in South Africa, the conversation eventually turns political. It may be wise to make your position clear from the start...

115

# MY ENTRY INTO THE REPUBLIC...

Jan Smuts Airport: Immigration. I present myself to a crisp and overly made up immigration officer. "Passport!" (no please) "Air Ticket" "Well I don't have one yet. I hope to get a cheap one in Jo'burg. I have plenty of cash, travellers cheques and credit cards..." Ding-a-wing-a-ling. She presses a little musical alert button ➡

This summons a yam-nosed goliath: the "problem case" superior. He listens with blinkered amiability. "Ya, ya", he understands... BUT... rules are rules. He explains the Republic's problem with bums and people who squander all their means. All manner of extremes ➡

"I'm not saying you'll do it..." he repeats this chorus. It is simply a matter of me leaving a 1200 Rand bond that I'm not a bum intending to inflict myself on the Republic. A non-negotiable "Welcome".
I arrive in Sunny S.A under a cloud ____

was shot at by some drunken soldiers of one of Africa's more sensible, black-run states.

A simple vehicle mishap becomes a racial incident. A black motorcyclist dares to vent anger at two leathery white dowagers with whom he has had a brush. '*What* did you say?'

I experience reverse racism. Denied entry to a convenient pale blue and dirt coloured 'black bus', I must hike to find a 'white' one. There is a black man aboard but he has authorisation. The driver checked. A drunken black trucker giving me a lift is into Jesus and booze, and in the market for a handgun. He screws me for a fare, but he screws the black riders too – fellows from his own tribe a little less so. Black truckers will brake for black hitchers, but won't for me. I try to avoid hitching near black hitchers as they are the kiss of death to a white BMW stopping.

Apartheid stinks. It is a loathsome scheme of 'separate development' that traffics in misery and panders to the most selfish and ignoble motives in man, contemptably disguised as altruism. *An unconscionable violation of fundamental human rights*, says the Canadian ambassador to the UN. It is unworkable in the long run. Even the chaps with the Alsatians and water cannons are beginning to realize that. They are wrong and they are in the minority, even among the whites.

South Africa is unlike anywhere else. It's easy to criticise and solve other people's problems when we haven't been there to be burdened with the realities and don't

In conversation, everyone tries to one-up one another in tales of racist monsters of their aquaintance.....

have to admit to our father's evils, nor live with the solutions. On taking a shortcut through the 'blacks only' section of the Johannesburg central rail station both the black crowds and I felt uncomfortable. I resented South Africa for a system that caused that saddening alienation.

Yet, the traveller's South Africa is an experience not always addled by the effects of apartheid. On the road I met memorable South Efs, black, brown and white, in a country that is a place of space and sinewy beauty under a peculiarly lit African sky.

I travelled in the 'R' months – OctobeR, NovembeR, DecembeR, when it's summer. Hitching, my face was burnt and my throat raw from the give-and-take talk about 'the Efs' and the country's future. I debated with South Africans of all colours of opinion and pigmentation. 'Charmaine and friend' dominated the non-racial conversation. She was a gorgeous blonde on sensational trial in Jo'burg for the multiple murders of lone hitchers.

*   *   *

Transkei is a South African contrivance; a nominally independent black state within the borders of the Republic. One of the myriad Rorschach inkblot 'homelands' blemishing the map of South Africa. It lies on the Indian coast, west of Durban, a stretch of raw and untamed beachfronts. Further west, the coast civilises into 'the Garden Route', gorgeous resortland exemplified by Plettenburg Bay. 'Plett. You're nobody 'till you've got a plot in Plett.'

I flagged down the Grim Boy Transport's Transkei local on the road outside Scottburg, near Durban, paying 8 Rand for a perch on the gearbox cover alongside the plexiglass-penned driver. I settled in, the only white face on the coach and the only one not smiling. It was to be an eight hour ride, the bus was raucous, ramshackle, replete; and frankly, it smelled bad.

The driver offered me a beer. He didn't like to drink alone, and most of the passengers were supping beers or home-brew as well. We fell into conversation through the porthole cut in his driving enclosure. A 'heated' conversation – the gearbox cover was commencing to grill my backside. 'You will like Transkei. Stick with me. We go by all the back ways. You see nothing on the motorway.' Tiko was his name and he called me 'Baba.' A wild-haired man with arms covered in nudie tattoos, Tico was outrageously gregarious over the roar of his engine and the *fsssst* of opening cans of beer.

He was a master wheelman, who would fling the bus off onto the verge in a shower of gravel to pick up hailing passengers and their inevitable mountains of effects. Livestock is mandatory in these situations and I wasn't disappointed. En route down the motorway BMW's and Mercedes sped toward the Wild Coast Holiday Inn and Casino, a self-styled sun and sin spot just over the 'border' from self-righteous South Africa. We did an end-around manoeuvre, and turned left into the Third World.

There were no border formalities or, if there were, no one noticed. I had troubled

"Lion of the mountains"

– a typical Transkei couple

On the Transkei Bus

to obtain a 'visa', but so what? The stops and starts for passengers were interspersed with pit stops. The radiator had a chronic leak and had to be topped up every hour or so. The driver sent his trio of assistants running down to seafront pools and streams to fetch buckets of water – evidently a regular routine as he knew all the locations by heart. The bus patrons would take these water-stop opportunities to pass a little water of their own in the wild grass among the dunes. As the bus pulled away, tailenders would scramble aboard hanging out the door like Keystone Cops.

Our coach, I had noticed, was Grim Boy Transport Service's 'Constellation State Tourer'. Its ambience was decidedly un-cosmic. Earthy. The menfolk on the bus were uniformly kitted out in Bogart fedoras and rummage sale winter overcoats. Many wore earrings in loops from dangling ear-lobes, and all carried knobkerries, the traditional sceptre-like skull crusher made out of a hardwood root. Some also carried umbrellas.

The women carried kids. There was not a woman of child bearing age who did not have evidence of this bound to her back with a heavy blanket. Often a lapful in front to balance the load. The women were Rubenesque and then some, padded out with blanket wrappers. The natural enemies of bus aisles.

No Third World bus trip is complete without (a) hair-raising cliff roads, (b) driving rain, (c) a lengthy breakdown (d) incomprehensible dramas among the passengers. We were not shortchanged.

"WHAT THE HELL DOES THAT MEAN!"...
NUMEROUS S.A. DRIVERS

The ubiquitous South African road crew flagman in orange overalls. He lashes his red warning flag randomly. Halt? Proceed? Go slow? Crash into the ditch? No one knew! The flagman least of all....

Every liberal South Africans "man who they don't care what color he is ( green with purple spots, etc...) they respect his right to self determination.

I'D BE TICKLED PINK WITH MY OWN HOMELAND

'We are entering Pondoland', said Tico, 'the stupidest people in Africa'. This with a touch of self effacement and a slosh of beer; he was himself a Pondo. We would be following 'the Dagga Route' a white-knuckle, cliffhanging route favoured by marijuana smugglers. Every year dope seized leaving Transkei exceeds that pseudo-nation's stated GNP. Tico, who seems to know, promises me a sampling of the 'cream of the crop' on arrival in Port St John's.

I would be delighted to settle for arrival; period. Tico manhandles the Constellation Tourer around increasingly precipitous cliff roads at a frantic pace, slowed not a bit by the doorknobs of rain that begin to fall. He is an affable bundle of outrageous confidence and lunatic bravado. These guys *always* are. After an ulcer-making hour it ceased to be terrifying. Faith. And more beers.

As the road grew more treacherous, the countryside grew more beautiful; sinuous, ruggedly-terraced and dappled by small villages; straw-thatched, mud-walled affairs. Goats and cattle on the nearby hillside. Villagers boarded with huge bags of wet cabbages and more babies. Up in the highlands (it did look almost Scottish), it was growing bitterly chilly and the people had little to smile about, but they all did. Or most. A comic opera battle ensued between two old women. It was all highly theatrical and they played to the crowd with overdone gestures and sense of ag-grievement. The men laughed and smoked. The women took sides. I slipped a couple

Ledgendary "Jack of the Bushveld" creating another homeland...

of paperbacks down the back of my jeans and sat back on the gearbox in silent and sizzling judgement.

We stopped for food. And more beer. It is not necessary to disembark; vendors lay siege to the coach and, fruit, loaves of bread and slabs of charred fish (unaesthetic but appetizing) are passed in through the windows. All the bones and every bit of litter goes on the floor. We became a mobile dump. But not for very long, as the bus suffered a breakdown. This was a signal for everyone to go to sleep except the babies. They screamed. Years of practice with makeshift mechanics and the threat of a good hammering got Grim Boy's Tourer on the road (at breakneck pace) again. Six hours into the journey it came to me that we looked like the aftermath of a bus wreck. Actual wreckage of buses far down the valley fostered this insight.

The rain cleared up, but not the mechanical maladies. At breakdown stops village kids came out to gawk from the hillsides. They do a kind of chorus line kick routine, clapping in sync beneath the kick leg. 'What's *that* mean?' 'Dunno', says the conductor. But I still suspect it may have been rude.

Transkei grew more and more rugged and beautiful. We followed the gorge of a boiling brown river, which funnels mists and huge flapping birds. All in all, a very 'Lost World' ambience. Finally the Indian Ocean was glimpsed, and it began to lash with rain again as we rolled into Port St John's. It's a tiny place, full of flower blossoms, where everyone knows Tico.

AFRIKAANS IS OF COURSE BAFFLING TO ANY VISITOR, BUT MUCH OF SOUTH AFRICAS PURPORTED ENGLISH IS MYSTERY TO ME...

'Mbochoga-ntaba' he is called – 'Lion of the Mountains'.

The Lion speaks. 'Did you like the ride? This is the best way to see Transkei. Don't worry, tomorrow you will be OK. I will put you on a bus with my friends (to Umtata, the capital) or you can hitch. No problem. You will get a ride tomorrow in a 350 SL Mercedes.'

And I did.

A ride to Ciskei. Evidence of the bogus nature of this nation of convenience for South Africa was found at the Ciskei Embassy in Durban. A pleasant receptionist didn't seem to mind the lack of furniture and squatted on the broadloom. The ambassador was delighted I'd come and gave me tea (no chair to sit on) and a visa he admitted was useless as Ciskei had no border post.

The Road takes me through 'the dorps' – small picture-perfect, country towns. Perfectly dull. They are thirsting through the pan-Africa drought of '83-'84. Conservation notices abound and 'Ankle Deep' are the bathwater bywords from Bitterfontein to Bugersdorp. But the drought breaks in southern Africa and I drive through hub-deep torrents to reach Underberg.

I do 'Durbs' (Durban), a place of English seaside vulgarity; 'The Cape' (Capetown), where 'the tablecloth' cloudbank descends on the city's Table Mountain, backdrop to the most beautiful city on earth. It does not obscure my view of Robbin Island penitentiary where every black leader worth a damn languishes.

I cross the Great Karoo. 'Miles and miles

THE FRIGHTENING THING, IS YOUR BLACKS DIDNT HAVE ANYTHING TO REBEL AGAINST THATS RHODESIA! WHAT WILL OUR ONES DO !?

Mr Rooster Take Away. Durban.

THIS IS THE GREATEST COUNTRY ON EARTH IF YOU'RE WHITE – THERES NO QUESTION ABOUT IT! ANYONE WHO SAYS DIFFERENT SHOULD BE LOCKED UP! PROVIDED YOU DONT THINK TOO DEEPLY YOU CAN GET ALONG – YOU HAVE TO BE PRETTY SUPERFICIAL.

Durban, Daily News, Durban

THERE'S NO NEED FOR MANY NEWSPAPERS HERE. THERE ARE ONLY FOUR PLACES WHERE ANYTHING EVER HAPPENS...

Beach Hotel Bar, Durban

of bugger all.' I pass the 'luxury valleys' of Paarl and Stellenbosch. I see the 'mattress people' of Crossroads, an illegal squatters' village where every morning they bury their plastic-and-stick houses under the sand and sit, smiling, on mattresses when the demolition teams arrive. I spend the night in 'hairyback heaven', Blemfontein, capital of the Orange Free State, something an Indian can't do by law . . . *What's the fastest thing in the Orange Free State? . . . An Indian on a bicycle!* I spend time in big, bad Jo'burg. And like it!

Lesotho (Leh-soo-too, home of the Bas-othos) is one of the *authentic* black states within South Africa. It is a happy place where everyone smells of horses. The other is Swaziland, where black, brown and white mix in harmony, and exist on subsistence agriculture, aid from South Africa and the proceeds of 'Happy Valley', a glitter gulch of casinos, sin spots, and sleaze, heavily patronized by Jo'burg weekenders. I book into the Jamilla Inn. 'Is this the cheapest hotel in Mbabane?' . . . 'It is the cheapest hotel in the *country*, sir!'

\*   \*   \*

The Zimbabwe ruins are like a jungle Stonehenge. Nobody knows exactly when they were built, but certainly before Cecil Rhodes invented Rhodesia. A local joke runs: 'In the past you went to Rhodesia to see the Zimbabwe ruins, now you go to Zimbabwe to see the Rhodesia ruins'.

\*   \*   \*

When you fly over Matabeleland it appears innocent enough. Look sharp and you might see elephants grazing. The land is flat, dusty, and not too heavily treed. But it *is* heavily Matabeled; the tribe who got the short end of the stick during the black power play in revolutionary ex-Rhodesia. At Victoria Falls airport the humidity hangs heavily as armed government troops salute the limp, multi-striped 'flying deck-chair' flag of the novice nation of Zimbabwe. (South-east Africa abounds in newly renamed revolutionary 'Z' countries and towns. Even the Republic of South Africa is being fitted with 'Azania', come the revolution.)

Soldiers man roadblocks on the Victoria Falls-Bulawayo road that runs by the airport. I am advised to beware of roadblock troops with curved magazines on their automatic weapons – these are Russian supplied 'AK somethings', the mark of Matabele insurgents ... You can't tell the players without a programme. A year before they had stopped an overland expedition truck and taken six backpackers, leaving no trace. This is headline land. Only three hours earlier I'd been in Jo'burg fitting myself for a snappy going home suit. I'd be home in four days. With luck!

*The week I wrote these lines, in the spring of '85, a news item buried in the international pages outlines the probable discovery of the six – their remains, buried in shallow graves.*

At the Victoria Falls Town Council Campsite and Chalet Park (up the stairs, across the tracks and under a train from

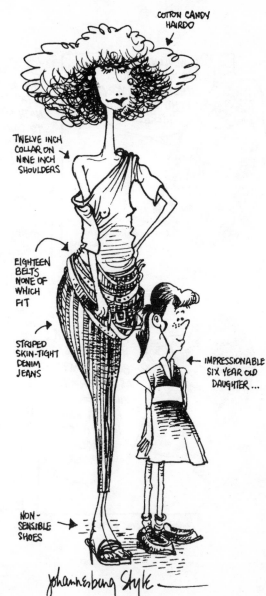

COTTON CANDY HAIRDO

TWELVE INCH COLLAR ON NINE INCH SHOULDERS

EIGHTEEN BELTS NONE OF WHICH FIT

STRIPED SKIN-TIGHT DENIM JEANS

IMPRESSIONABLE SIX YEAR OLD DAUGHTER ...

NON-SENSIBLE SHOES

Johannesburg Style

Guide to Johannesburg:

Highbrow

Hillbrow

the rail depot) I re-encountered Dave. On my three-day fly-in junket from Jo'burg, I was almost a tourist. When I bade him goodbye again, I passed the traveller's baton. He would be on the road for another 14 months, and I would travel vicariously through his postcards.

*No commercialism is allowed to spoil this natural wonder* – quote from a Zimbabwe government tourist brochure. There are pathways of crushed indigenous rock at Vic Falls, charmingly ineffectual barriers of brambles, worrysome wild warthogs and other natural wonders, but in 1983 there was very, very little water. It is possible to walk right along the lip of much of what was once waterfall. The mile long chasm walls have only fingers of water cascading over much of their length. The drought. Mother Nature was having to make do with 'Ankle Deep' also.

Still, from the Zambian side particularly, the spray constantly rains upward making this a place of perpetual rainbows and a spot for sodden introspection. The pot of gold at the rainbow's end was, in this case, an Israeli under an umbrella with a friendly line of chat, a pressing need for foreign exchange, and a medical bag full of Zimbabwean notes. Dave and I blackmarketed at the edge of one of the seven natural wonders of the world. Just add water and stir.

\* \* \*

My last night in Africa, my last night as a traveller to date, was spent alone in the

I WOULDNT WALK AROUND SOWETO... THEY'RE NOT VERY FOND OF US OUT THERE.

Government Tourist Office, Carlton Centre, Johannesburg

YOU KNOW, AS SOMEONE WHO COMES FROM THIS PART OF THE WORLD YOU DON'T KNOW WHAT TO SAY... SO YOU SAY NOTHING. I JUST TELL THEM TO COME TO SOUTH AFRICA AND DECIDE FOR THEMSELVES.

Claim Street, Hillbrow, Johannesburg

YOU CAN ALWAYS TELL AN EX – RHODIE ... THEY NEVER WEAR SOCKS !!

Café Wien, Johannesburg

THIS IS FRANK; HIS NAME IS BOTHA, SAME AS THE PRIME MINISTER ... HE'S A REAL HAIRYBACK; A ROCK SPIDER ...

Phoenix Hotel Bar, Barberton, SA.

I DON'T BLAME THE ANC. I DON'T! THEY'VE TALKED AND TALKED AND TALKED AND TALKED 'TILL THEY WERE BLACK IN THE FACE....

Berea, Johannesburg, SA

Cafe Wien on Kotze St, Johannesburg, where many of the South African drawings in this book were completed. They have a small, arm-chaired screening room there, and I watched Vincent Price in *Theatre of Death*. I had arranged a date with a girl I'd met a week earlier, but I lost the address she had written inside the cover of a paperback novel. I had unthinkingly given the book to a border soldier on the Zambian side of the frontier at Vic Falls. This too, is travelling; you're sublime, you're ridiculous, and everything in between, but above all you are living . . . on the Road.

The next morning, I flew home. I thought back fondly to places like Nelspruit, Arusha, Nboka, and Bafwasende from 'this trip'; to Koh Samui, Ngadisari, Varanasi and Orange from the 'last one!' And I thought of the people who fill this book, and who fill my recollections. An ending. But not quite. My travels end at home, if they end at all. They are memories, learned experiences to make the present interlude more pleasant, and to make plans for new ones. For the next time! . . . . On the Road.

\*    \*    \*

**Lonely Planet travel guides**

*Africa on a Shoestring*
*Australia – a travel survival kit*
*Alaska – a travel survival kit*
*Bali & Lombok – a travel survival kit*
*Burma – a travel survival kit*
*Bushwalking in Papua New Guinea*
*Canada – a travel survival kit*
*China – a travel survival kit*
*Hong Kong, Macau & Canton*
*India – a travel survival kit*
*Japan – a travel survival kit*
*Kashmir, Ladakh & Zanskar*
*Kathmandu & the Kingdom of Nepal*
*Korea & Taiwan – a travel survival kit*
*Malaysia, Singapore & Brunei – a travel survival kit*
*Mexico – a travel survival kit*
*New Zealand – a travel survival kit*
*North-East Asia on a Shoestring*
*Pakistan – a travel survival kit*
*Papua New Guinea – a travel survival kit*
*The Philippines – a travel survival kit*
*South America on a Shoestring*
*South-East Asia on a Shoestring*
*Sri Lanka – a travel survival kit*
*Thailand – a travel survival kit*
*Tramping in New Zealand*
*Travellers Tales*
*Trekking in the Nepal Himalaya*
*USA West*
*West Asia on a Shoestring*

**Lonely Planet phrasebooks**

*Indonesia Phrasebook*
*China Phrasebook*
*Nepal Phrasebook*
*Thailand Phrasebook*

Lonely Planet travel guides are available around the world. If you can't find them, ask your bookshop to order them from one of the distributors listed below. For countries not listed or if you would like a free copy of our latest booklist write to Lonely Planet in Australia.

**Australia**
Lonely Planet Publications, PO Box 88, South Yarra, Victoria 3141.

**Canada** see USA

**Denmark**
Scanvik Books aps, Store Kongensgade 59 A, DK-1264 Copenhagen K.

**Hong Kong**
The Book Society, GPO Box 7804.

**India & Nepal**
UBS Distributors, 5 Ansari Rd, New Delhi.

**Israel**
Geographical Tours Ltd, 8 Tverya St, Tel Aviv 63144.

**Japan**
Intercontinental Marketing Corp, IPO Box 5056, Tokyo 100-31.

**Malaysia**
MPH Distributors, 13 Jalan 13/6, Petaling Jaya, Selangor.

**Netherlands**
Nilsson & Lamm bv, Postbus 195, Pampuslaan 212, 1380 AD Weesp.

**New Zealand**
Roulston Greene Publishing Associates Ltd, Box 33850, Takapuna, Auckland 9.

**Pakistan**
London Book House, 281/C Tariq Rd, PECHS Karachi 29, Pakistan

**Papua New Guinea** see Australia

**Singapore**
MPH Distributors, 3rd Storey, 601 Sims Drive #03-21, Singapore 1438

**Spain**
Altair, Riera Alta 8, Barcelona, 08001.

**Sweden**
Esselte Kartcentrum AB, Vasagatan 16, S-111 20 Stockholm.

**Thailand**
Chalermnit, 108 Sukhumvit 53, Bangkok, 10110.

**UK**
Roger Lascelles, 47 York Rd, Brentford, Middlesex, TW8 0QP.

**USA**
Lonely Planet Publications, PO Box 2001A, Berkeley, CA 94702.

**West Germany**
Buchvertrieb Gerda Schettler, Postfach 64, D3415 Hattorf a H.